CW00348763

ADVANCE PRAISE FOR *ON THE NOSE*

"Hans Florine is a living legend and a gifted storyteller. You don't need to be a climber to be drawn into the majestic history and adventure that encompass Yosemite's El Capitan."

—Rebecca Rusch, seven-time world-champion
endurance athlete and author of *Rusch to Glory*

"Over the course of 101 ascents of America's most iconic climbing route—the Nose—Hans Florine has inspired young and old with his motivation and pure love of life."

—Phil Powers, CEO of the American Alpine Club

"Hans Florine actually helps others to beat his records—simply because it motivates everyone to keep improving. I've never met a person with such a drive to inspire, encourage, and help others succeed. His book is an energizing journey filled with powerful lessons on personal leadership, effectiveness, and ways to encourage ourselves and others to continuously improve."

—Rich Fettke, cofounder of Real Wealth Network, Inc.,
and author of *Extreme Success*

"Hans Florine's book about climbing El Capitan is a captivating study not just on the history of bold Yosemite climbing, but into the modern climber's mind-set. His voice is at once commanding and intriguing . . . hard to put this book down once you dive in."

—Kenji Haroutunian, VP/director of Outdoor Retailer trade shows, 2007–2014

"Hans's commitment to the Nose route on El Capitan is like Dale Carnegie's commitment to influencing people. He won't stop until he 'owns it'—rivals become partners, acquaintances in the climbing community become vested in the joy of the ascent, and everyone, every ascent, becomes a positive learning experience."

—Chris Widener, motivational speaker and author

"This book will captivate all who read it."

—Fiona Thornewill, world record–setting polar explorer

"Hans Florine has mastered the Nose through a combination of talent, fitness, and ruthless efficiency. His speed-climbing records inspire us to reimagine what's possible. All climbers—from slow-and-steady novices to one-day speedsters—will enjoy this book."

—Mark Kroese, author of *Fifty Favorite Climbs: The Ultimate North American Tick List*

"Speed-climber extraordinaire Hans Florine is a rare individual. *On the Nose* cracks open the world of this remarkable man and lays bare his 30-year love affair with Yosemite's El Capitan that has driven him to climb the 3,000-foot-tall monolith more than a hundred times and set a series of ever more amazing speed records. Exciting, inspiring, jaw-dropping, and a ton of fun."

—Gregory Crouch, author of *Enduring Patagonia* and *China's Wings*

"*On the Nose* is a joyous read through the history of the Nose speed record. Hans's laid-back, modest, self-deprecating style makes the book flow easily, and I tore through it at Hollywood-Hans pace. I came away inspired and learned a valuable lesson: Find your passion, find what you excel at, and drive it to the very limit of your abilities."

—Bill Wright, climber, adventurer, author

"Lean, strong, with just the right amount of soul. So is his book. Hans Florine's insightful memoir, *On the Nose*, allows even those who think nuts are edible and ascenders are upwardly mobile socialites to experience the challenge of climbing Yosemite's most iconic big wall."

—Kristi Denton Cohen, director of *Vertical Frontier*

"What I love about Hans Florine's new book is that he has watched history unfold on the Nose and has been right in the thick of that history. The story of this famous rock face is a microcosm of the modern world in its quest for speed and inexorable progress."

—Erik Weihenmayer, only blind person to climb the Seven Summits

"I literally could not put the book down. Hans covers a lot of ground very succinctly, perhaps somewhat akin to the way he climbs the Nose. And for those who like love stories, it has that, too. But what really brought tears to my eyes was the way his book brought home so forcefully that there are still people out there who aspire to excel, to break barriers, to dedicate themselves to the impossible dream."

—George Whitmore, first ascent of El Capitan, 1958

"I have always admired how Hans embraces competition as a universal way we can help each other become the best we can be, rather than a way to rise above others. Though he clearly knows how to 'rise above' in many ways, he does so with kindness, puppy-like enthusiasm, and goodwill. I recommend this book to anyone interested in California rock climbing, how to live a passionate life, friendship, and what the human body and spirit can accomplish."

—Amelia Rudolph, founder of Bandaloop vertical dance troupe

"What this book makes clear is that the race for the Nose speed record ranks right up there with the Kentucky Derby and the Daytona 500 as one of the greatest sports dramas on earth. And for magnitude of venue, El Cap wins hands down."

—John Long, legendary climber and author

"Hans Florine's lifelong obsession with the Nose route on El Capitan has no parallel in modern outdoor sport. It would qualify as insane if El Capitan were not so mysteriously beautiful, and if the Nose route itself were not so endlessly compelling. No cliff on earth matches the skills and yearnings of the contemporary rock climber in quite the way that El Capitan does, and no other climber has so dedicated himself to mastering and, more importantly, enjoying the gift of this great rock over multiple decades. This book is the story of that ongoing love affair, and what a story it is!"

—Daniel Duane, author of seven books including
El Capitan: Historic Feats and Radical Routes

"Much like my own passion and obsession with ever increasing the mind's ability to remember, Hans has focused on ever improving his speed on the most prized route on the most famous granite cliff in all of climbing. The stories he shares on some of his 101 ascents are inspiring, so much so you won't need any of my memory tricks to remember them!"

—Ron White, two-time national memory champion

"Hans has been personally involved in nearly every major climbing milestone played out on the Nose of El Capitan over the last 30 years. For anyone with any interest in the history and mythology of one of the greatest rock climbs in the world, *On the Nose* is a must-read."

—Brady Robinson, executive director of the Access Fund

"Hans Florine is a true legend in the climbing community, and this book is a fascinating account of his continuing drive and dedication to climbing the Nose route on El Capitan—great reading for everybody who loves adventure, passion, and Yosemite National Park."

—Scott Gediman, public affairs officer, Yosemite National Park

"*On the Nose* is as inspirational as it is gripping, and it reveals many powerful clues for success—in both the vertical and the everyday worlds."

—Eric J. Hörst, author of international bestseller *Training for Climbing*

"Our seven-day ascent of the Nose was five weeks faster than the first ascent. We thought that was pretty good, but Hans's and Alex's time of 2:23:46 is in a different league in terms of climbing skills and boldness. Hans's story is world-class, much like the man himself, who does everything with integrity, focus, and dedication—always right on the Nose."

—Tom Frost, second ascent of the Nose, 1960

"In *On the Nose*, Hans Florine chronicles nearly three decades of obsession—his personal story provides a deeply informative view of what it takes to ascend the world's most famous rock climb, as well as life within the climbing community that orbits around Yosemite National Park."

—Mike Gauthier, chief of staff, Yosemite National Park

"It was fun to read *On the Nose* and realize how many people's lives (and climbers' careers) Hans has inspired through his passionate pursuit of the Nose route on El Capitan. I'm so glad to have been among the first 10 of Hans's 101 ascents. This book is a must-read for anyone seeking to live out their passions."

—Lynn Hill, world-champion climber, first free ascent of the Nose

"No one on planet earth knows more about the Nose, the most striking line up the most beautiful granite wall on the earth, than Hans Florine. His love affair with this iconic climb is borne of the kind of dogged obsession that makes for the best kind of climbing stories."

—Nick Rosen, Sender Films

ON THE NOSE

A LIFELONG OBSESSION WITH
YOSEMITE'S MOST ICONIC CLIMB

HANS FLORINE
WITH JAYME MOYE

Guilford, Connecticut
Helena, Montana

An imprint of Rowman & Littlefield

Falcon and FalconGuides are registered trademarks and Make Adventure Your Story is a trademark of Rowman & Littlefield.

Distributed by NATIONAL BOOK NETWORK

Copyright © 2016 Hans Florine and Jayme Moye

All rights reserved. No part of this book may be reproduced in any form or by any electronic or mechanical means, including information storage and retrieval systems, without written permission from the publisher, except by a reviewer who may quote passages in a review.

British Library Cataloguing in Publication Information available

Library of Congress Cataloging-in-Publication Data

Names: Florine, Hans, author. | Moye, Jayme, co-author.
Title: On the Nose : a lifelong obsession with Yosemite's most iconic climb /
   Hans Florine and Jayme Moye.
Description: Guilford, Connecticut : Falcon, [2016]
Identifiers: LCCN 2016018748 (print) | LCCN 2016020256 (ebook) | ISBN
   9781493024988 (hardcover : alkaline paper) | ISBN 9781493024995 (e-book)
Subjects: LCSH: Florine, Hans. | Mountaineering—California—Yosemite
   National Park—History. | El Capitan (Calif.)—Description and travel. |
   Yosemite National Park (Calif.)—Description and travel. |
   Mountaineers—California—Yosemite National Park—Biography. | Yosemite
   National Park (Calif.)—Biography.
Classification: LCC GV199.42.C22 Y67187 2017 (print) | LCC GV199.42.C22
   (ebook) | DDC 796.522092 [B] —dc23
LC record available at https://lccn.loc.gov/2016018748

♾™ The paper used in this publication meets the minimum requirements of American National Standard for Information Sciences—Permanence of Paper for Printed Library Materials, ANSI/NISO Z39.48-1992.

CONTENTS

INTRODUCTION

El Capitan is awe-inspiring. I've watched visitors to Yosemite National Park who, upon seeing the granite cliff for the first time, gasp, their eyes welling with tears. I've seen others, including young children, become inexplicably still in its presence. Part of the magic of El Capitan is its size—3,000 vertical feet of lustrous rock, soaring above the trees like a castle or a cathedral. And part of it is its accessibility. The base of El Capitan is a 15-minute walk from your car. There are few places on earth where you can get to such a wild, colossal rock face without first renting a floatplane, or a Russian helicopter, and perhaps a yak.

The fact that we've figured out how to climb El Capitan—and therefore how to have a personal relationship with it—makes it all the more remarkable. It's not a stretch to say that climbing El Cap, typically a three- to five-day endeavor, ranks among the greatest adventures of our time. Since the first ascent in 1958, thousands have attempted El Capitan, most via the Nose route, which is the original line following the cliff's massive prow.

About 64 percent make it to the top. The others, overcome by fear, vertigo, fatigue, dehydration, and sometimes injury, are forced to rappel—descend by rope—to the bottom or accept a helicopter evacuation. The Nose is considered the ultimate proving ground for big-wall climbers.

I first climbed the Nose in 1989. It took me and a college buddy 46 hours of continuous climbing, interspersed with a couple naps wherever we could find a ledge wide enough to rest on. By then a couple of the best Yosemite climbers in the world had figured out how to climb the route in under 24 hours. "Nose in a Day," or NIAD, was the mark to achieve.

Today, the fastest time up the Nose remains the most coveted speed record in climbing and has been called the wildest competition on earth. In my thirty-year quest to lay claim to that record, I've had the privilege of partnering with (and competing against) some of the most storied names in modern climbing—Peter Croft, Steve Schneider, Timmy O'Neill, Dean Potter, Yuji Hirayama, Tommy Caldwell, Thomas and Alexander Huber, Sean Leary, and, most recently, Alex Honnold—to whittle the time it takes to climb the Nose down to a mind-blowing 2 hours, 23 minutes, and 46 seconds.

Professional climbers, myself included, continue to push the limits of what's possible on El Capitan. Our most remarkable achievements—like when Tommy Caldwell and Kevin Jorgeson made the first free ascent of El Capitan's ridiculously sheer Dawn Wall in 2015—capture mainstream media attention to a degree never before experienced in the history of rock climbing. More news stories, magazine articles, and documentary films have been created about El Capitan than anything else in the sport. It's become the most famous vertical wall in the world.

I've had the idea of writing a book about my experiences on El Cap for a while now. I figured the topic would interest at least a subsegment of the population (mainly other climbers). But it wasn't until September 12, 2015, when I made my one hundredth ascent of the Nose, that I felt compelled to write this book, and to do it for a larger audience.

I realized then how ludicrous it is that I've climbed the Nose one hundred times. And how equally ridiculous it is that I have no intention of stopping anytime soon. I'm not a young man anymore. I'm married with two kids, have more than a full-time job managing a rock-climbing gym in the San Francisco Bay Area, and speak and teach all over the world. Yet I can't give up the Nose.

This book is my best attempt to answer the question why. I hope it will lead to some interesting insights about how to live a satisfying life, how to achieve big goals, and how an otherwise ordinary guy can become a rock star.

—Hans Florine

PROLOGUE

El Capitan was born of fire. The 3,000-foot-tall, 1.5-mile-wide sheer granite cliff rising up from present-day Yosemite Valley in central California started forming roughly 220 million years ago, when ancestral North America collided with a neighboring tectonic plate underlying the Pacific Ocean. The slow, grinding impact forced the Pacific plate beneath what is now California, igniting a subterranean pressure cooker that liquefied the earth's deepest rock layers into red-hot magma.

The buoyant molten rock seeped upward through the earth's crust for miles, forming the bowels of an ancient chain of volcanoes, not unlike the modern-day Andes. Some of it erupted skyward—apocalyptical blasts far more powerful than anything experienced in recorded human history—then spread out and cooled. Traces of volcanic ash can still be found in the rock layers below the surface of central North America, a testament to the breadth of the eruptions.

The vast majority of the magma, however, remained underground, where it slowly cooled and, over many eons, crystallized into granite—one of the toughest natural materials known to man. Granite, an igneous rock with large interlocking crystals of various minerals, mainly quartz and feldspar, is as strong as steel and twice as hard as marble.

So El Capitan began, part of an otherwise undifferentiated mass in a subterranean granite reserve, or batholith, spanning 400 miles in length and 100 miles in width. And there it would have remained, had tectonic pressures some 10 million years ago not resulted in a fault system along the batholith's eastern edge. Uplift eventually ratcheted the batholith to the surface, where it would become the most recognizable part of California's Sierra Nevada mountain range.

Much as Renaissance sculptors freed human forms from lifeless marble, erosion painstakingly carved El Capitan from the Sierra Nevada. Over the course of tens of millions of years, the ancestral Merced River, draining high from the Sierras, shaped the valley that would become Yosemite, chipping away the weaker rock between El Capitan and the earth's surface to uncover the colossal cliff face we can see today.

But it wasn't until the most recent ice age, about three million years ago, that glaciers rolled through Yosemite Valley and put the finishing touches on El Capitan, setting it up to become the rock-climbing world's most famous "big wall." First, the glaciers widened Yosemite Valley itself, changing its shape from a river-carved V to an ice-carved U. This scraped out all the rock previously covering the base of El Capitan, exposing its full 3,000-foot height. Next, the slow-moving masses of ice scavenged any loose structures from the cliff's face, creating a stark, vertical wall. Finally, the glaciers polished the granite that was left behind, etching a multitude of microscopic scratches in the rock's surface that reflect light, giving the rock face a luminous glow.

With the retreat of the glaciers some 15,000 years ago, the granite of El Capitan expanded; a natural release after having been subject to the pressure of the ice, which topped several hundred pounds per square inch under the largest glaciers. This geologic exhale shot slivers of cracks through the cliff, particularly at its prow joining the southwest and southwest faces. These slivers weren't nearly enough to compromise the granite's integrity but, as humans eventually discovered, were large enough to use as handholds and footholds.

The first humans to gaze upon El Capitan, and the lesser granite formations of Yosemite Valley, were likely the Ahwahneechee Indians, a subgroup of the Miwok tribe, who lived in the western Sierras for thousands of years after the glaciers receded. They called the bountiful valley *Ahwahnee*, "Place Like a Gaping Mouth." They hunted wild game, fished the Merced River, and harvested more than one hundred types of edible plants.

El Capitan stood like an unfailing sentinel on the south flank of the valley, cleaving the lush 7-mile span in two roughly equal halves. Native American names for the rock formation varied. In some reports the cliff was called *To-tock-ah-noo-lah*, translated as "the Rock Chief." Others knew it as *To-to-kon oo-lah*, "the Sandhill Crane," after the chief of the First People. Still others said *Tul-tok-a-nu-la*, which originated from an old myth about the measuring worm (*tul-tok-a-na*), which rescued two young boys stranded on the cliff by crawling up the face of the rock.

Juan Rodriguez Cabrillo, the first European to explore California, sailed from Mexico in 1542. But it wasn't until 1851, more than three centuries later, that white men would "discover" El Capitan. The Gold Rush of 1849 had lured thousands of fortune-seekers into the Sierra Nevada. After the Miwok began repelling these interlopers, the new state of California hired bounty hunters and private militias to exterminate the region's indigenous people.

On March 21, 1851, a 200-man battalion purposed with "reclaiming" the land reached an overlook with views of Yosemite Valley. This was the first time a white man had laid eyes on El Capitan. The battalion forced the Ahwahneechee to a reservation west of the mountains. Shortly after, Yosemite's original residents received special permission from the state to return, but life in the valley was never the same, and their numbers soon dwindled.

In 1855, four years after the battalion's discovery, James Hutchings, an adventurous newspaper reporter, came across an account of its travels. Intrigued by the tales of 1,000-foot-high waterfalls and rock cliffs, he set out with two Indian guides on a five-day exploratory expedition. His resulting article about "Yo-Semity," published in a Mariposa, California, newspaper, described a "singular and romantic valley" of "wild and sublime grandeur."

The next year two ambitious miners opened a 50-mile horse trail leading into Yosemite Valley. The first hotel, a rustic retreat with dirt floors and no panes in the windows, opened in 1857.

El Capitan's earliest admirers were more interested in evoking the mighty rock cliff's likeness in paintings than in scaling it. Landscape painter Albert Bierstadt arrived in Yosemite in 1863. He wrote to a friend that he had found the Garden of Eden. Bierstadt's painting *Looking Down on Yosemite Valley*, featuring El Capitan, established him as one of America's top landscape artists.

Even by then, only a few hundred people had seen Yosemite Valley in person. But the area had captured enough of the public imagination through art and journalism that President Abraham Lincoln signed a bill to create the Yosemite Grant, a state-owned land trust to preserve Yosemite for future generations.

Near the end of the nineteenth century, conservationists led by naturalist and author John Muir began pushing for the area to become a national park. No doubt Muir was thinking of El Capitan when he penned his impassioned articles extolling Yosemite's grandeur for the *Century Magazine*: "No temple made with hands can compare to Yosemite." In 1906 President Theodore Roosevelt, after camping for several days with Muir in Yosemite's backcountry, signed a bill to transfer the Yosemite Land Grant to the National Park Service.

In 1916 Yosemite National Park inspired a young man who would go on to become one of the most influential photographers of all time. Ansel Adams was just 14 when his family traveled from their home in San Francisco to visit the park. At the entrance his father presented him with a life-changing gift: a Kodak Brownie box camera. Over the next six decades, Adams's black-and-white photographs of the American West, especially Yosemite, elevated photography to an art form comparable with painting and music. Among his greatest works is *El Capitan, Winter, Sunrise, Yosemite National Park, California*, a 20-by-16-inch portrait of a cloud-shrouded El Capitan, glistening white with snow. Instead of a stark, powerful rock cliff in shades of granite gray, Adams's masterpiece shows a soft, ethereal El Capitan, partially shrouded in clouds and glistening white with snow.

It wasn't until the 1940s, nearly a century after Yosemite entered the American consciousness, that human interactions with El Capitan turned tactile. After World War II, the availability of inexpensive army surplus climbing ropes and camping gear inspired mountaineers to begin exploring Yosemite's many towering buttresses, spires, and turrets.

Throughout the 1940s and '50s, climbers worked their way up Yosemite's towering granite formations by pounding pitons, metal spikes with an eye-hole on one end to attach a rope, up the wall as they went. The ability to navigate the sheer magnitude of Yosemite's cliffs forged a visceral connection between man and rock unlike anything experienced before. Yosemite Valley became the "big-wall" climbing capital of the world. But its biggest wall, El Capitan, presumed impossible to scale for its height and verticality, would remain untouched for nearly two more decades.

In the summer of 1957, an audacious American named Warren Harding began the first attempt to climb El Capitan. He applied mountaineering techniques used in the Himalayas, fixing ropes between "camps" along El Capitan's monumental prow, which would come to be known as the Nose. The ascent required a small team of men 45 days of work, spread out over 18 months, to piece together a plausible route up, finally reaching the top in freezing weather on November 12, 1958.

Others would later refine Harding's techniques, figuring out ways to scale the Nose faster and more efficiently. Advances in climbing gear and the creation of sticky rubber-soled shoes would enable more than just a band of hard-core mountaineers to put hand and foot to El Capitan. Today, "sending the Nose" requires only a three- to five-day effort for experienced climbers, and less than a day for the world's elite.

Over the last half century, climbers have created dozens of additional routes up El Capitan on both sides of the Nose. Still, retracing Harding's original ascent remains one of the world's great outdoor challenges.

One climber, Hans Florine, knows El Capitan more intimately than any other human ever has, and perhaps ever will. On September 12, 2015, the California resident made his record-setting 100th ascent of the Nose, bringing his total number of El Capitan ascents to 160. Call it obsession, call it destiny, this is his story.

CHAPTER I

Virgin Time

I was pretty sure I was about to die. One second before, I'd been standing on a piton, a metal spike wedged into a granite rock face some 300 feet above the Yosemite Valley floor. Suddenly the piton had shifted, causing me to lose my balance. I pawed frantically at the rock wall to steady myself. Before I could catch either my breath or my balance, the piton dislodged completely, taking me with it. As I began to fall, I squeezed my eyes shut. This was it.

Less than 24 hours earlier, I'd been speeding northward along California State Route 41, my college roommate Mike Lopez at the wheel and me riding shotgun in a pair of Big Dog volleyball shorts and no shirt. July of 1988 was a scorcher, with temperatures regularly hitting 100°F. It didn't help that the air conditioner in Mike's ancient Chevy Nova was busted. That summer, which later became known as the opening salvo of a historic five-year drought, we spent considerably more hours roasting in his car driving to national parks to rock-climb than we did job hunting following our graduation from California Polytechnic State University in San Luis Obispo.

On that particular weekend we were headed to Yosemite. It was to be both my and Mike's first ascent of the Nose route on El Capitan—arguably the most famous rock climb on the planet. It doesn't matter if you learn to climb at the Cleveland Rock Gym in Euclid, Ohio, or in Eldorado Canyon in Boulder, Colorado, or in my case, on a big boulder in the middle of the cow field in San Luis Obispo, California. Sooner or later you'll hear about the 3,000-foot granite cliff that presides over Yosemite Valley. There have been more books, films, and general campfire lore generated about El Cap than anything else in climbing. The same way that Mount Everest draws the world's most adventurous mountaineers, El Capitan lures the world's greatest rock climbers, along with wannabes like me and Mike.

In my five years of climbing, I'd gotten the sense that there were really only two kinds of climbers in California—the ones who were good enough to climb the Nose and the ones who weren't. I was ready to find out to which side I belonged.

Besides being a proving ground, climbing the Nose is also a pilgrimage. During prior trips to Yosemite, I'd come to understand that climbing demands a certain reverence for its history. Climbers, *real* climbers anyway, speak of the sport's early pioneers, like Royal Robbins and Warren Harding, the way nonclimbers speak of George Washington and Thomas Jefferson. Real climbers know and respect Yosemite as the birthplace of big-wall climbing and consider its first ascents sacred. If climbing were a religion, sending the Nose would be like getting baptized.

Hurling along the highway with Mike, I wasn't thinking such heady thoughts. I was trying to get the crappy FM radio to pick up the hard rock station coming out of Fresno. I'd grown bored of listening to Pink Floyd's *The Wall*, which was the only undamaged cassette tape that Mike seemed to own. The radio offered no reprieve—lots of fuzz, punctuated by an occasional riff from Black Sabbath. I gave up and punched it off.

That left talking, or yelling actually, over the rush of wind through the open windows. I'm pretty sure we talked about what we always talked about on climbing road trips: other climbers. And since we were gunning for the Nose on El Cap, our subject was surely Warren Harding, the first person to climb it.

The way the story goes, rock climbers began exploring Yosemite in the 1940s and even more so after World War II. By the late 1950s they had scaled all the major formations and rock walls there—except El Capitan. It was considered the most technical rock climb ever conceived, for both its steepness and its length. Many claimed it wasn't possible. In fact, it wasn't until 1958—five years *after* Tenzing Norgay and Edmund Hillary claimed the first summit of Mount Everest—that El Cap saw its first ascent.

The man responsible for the expedition—I call it an expedition because it took forty-five days over the span of eighteen months—went by the nickname "Batso." Warren Harding stood just 5 feet tall, but his intense blue eyes, thick crop of dark hair, and devil-may-care demeanor made him seem larger than life.

Harding set up camp in Yosemite in the summer of 1957 and, along with a small team of friends, began fixing ropes on El Capitan. The sight of climbers dangling on the wall astonished tourists and caused so many traffic jams on the single road through the park that the Park Service initially shut the project down. Allegedly, a ranger stood in the meadow with a bullhorn and bellowed, "Get your ass down!" It was only after Harding agreed to work on the ascent exclusively during the park's off-season (before Memorial Day and after Labor Day) that he was allowed to resume.

In the car Mike and I bantered around tales we'd heard of Harding during our earlier visits to Yosemite. He was bold, controversial, and more often drunk than not. Yet his talent was unmistakable. Of all the words used to describe Harding, who died at age 77 in 2002, the one that resonates most with me is "visionary." The guy pulled off the biggest wall of them all, in a world where so-called big-wall climbing didn't really even exist yet.

The right gear for what Harding aspired to hadn't even been created. There weren't even plastic water bottles. He and his team used motor-oil cans to hold their water. They lugged up hammers to bang metal spikes called pitons into cracks in the wall. In comparison, the nuts, hexes, and spring-loaded camming devices that Mike and I would carry were featherweight and slid easily into cracks, no pounding required. And they were amazingly strong. You could hang a VW bus—the climber's car of choice—off one tiny nut. We also had far better climbing shoes and significantly stronger ropes.

I don't know if Harding deliberated over what section of El Cap to climb or not. The cliff is about a mile wide, so he had a lot of options. I like to think he was immediately drawn to the Nose—El Cap's massive prow—because it would have been the most audacious choice. It's pretty much smack in the center, jutting out like the beak of a parrot. And it's visible from any vantage point in the park.

The Nose wasn't a choice for me. If you're going to climb El Cap, you've got to climb Harding's original line up the prow. Mike and I knew that much. What we didn't know was that most teams set aside three to five days to send the Nose. Whether it was ignorance or arrogance, or some combination of the two, we were planning to climb it over the weekend.

"We should try to make it to Dolt Tower on the first day," Mike said. He didn't have to yell because I'd rolled the windows up—a game I'd just invented to see how long we could stand the stifling heat in a car with no air conditioner.

I considered Mike's statement as the car morphed into a mobile sauna. The Nose is 3,000 vertical feet, which climbers break up into thirty-one pitches. A pitch is roughly a 100-foot section that can be completed within one rope's length. Dolt Tower is at the top of pitch 11, or about one-third of the way up. Part of the appeal, besides that it put us on track to top out after 2.5 days of climbing, was Dolt Tower's natural ledge. We couldn't afford portaledges—the ultra-secure structures that climbers anchor to vertical walls to sleep for the night—so the ledge would provide a relatively flat, comfortable place to sleep. "Yeah, that would be ideal," I said, wiping sweat from my forehead.

Of course, there was always the risk that the ledge we planned to sleep on would already be taken. "We should start really early so we get to Dolt Tower first," I added, glancing at Mike. He nodded, his face pink from the heat. Mike knew about my unsavory experience in Yosemite last summer. I was climbing the Salathé Wall with a friend of my sister's, and as dusk faded to dark, we couldn't find a ledge to sleep on, so we just kept going. Eventually, our bodies and brains gave out—or gave in, rather. We slept hanging on the wall, seated in our harnesses. Both my legs went totally numb.

I hoped we wouldn't have to resort to such tactics on the Nose. Mike grumbled something about not being able to breathe with the windows up. Apparently our combined body odor was killing him as much as the heat. I was lost in my own thoughts about the Nose. I knew that big-wall climbing was a sufferfest. The Nose wouldn't be easy. It probably wouldn't even be all that fun. It was just something I had to do if I wanted to call myself a rock climber, a *real* rock climber. I rolled down the window and the air rushed back in. Mike breathed a sigh of relief.

Neither of us ever considered that the climb could go catastrophically wrong.

The sun was still high in the sky when Mike and I pulled into the parking lot at Camp 4, the closest legal campsite to the base of El Capitan, which was 2.6 miles down the road. Since we didn't have real jobs yet, we'd left early on Friday. Pretty much everyone else in the San Francisco and Los Angeles metropolitan areas was still at work when we pulled into Camp 4, which assured us one of the coveted camping spots.

The next day we woke at 4:30 a.m. I wore the cotton shirt I'd slept in, changed my shorts to tights, and yanked on a pair of kneepads—which would hopefully protect my knees from banging against 3,000 feet worth of granite. We threw down a quick breakfast of bagels and soda and jumped in the car. It was understood that we needed to move fast if we wanted to secure Dolt Tower. We sped to El Cap Meadow and hurriedly began the 15-minute walk through the woods to the base.

Against the predawn sky El Capitan loomed so large it blocked out the stars. We hiked the path to the base wearing headlamps. As we got deeper into the woods, gnarled manzanita trees and craggy boulders lined the route like warlocks and trolls. The path became increasingly rocky, littered with chunks of granite that had calved off the Nose in a colossal earthquake-induced rockfall some 3,600 years ago. The hike would have felt surreal, kind of Middle Earth–esque, had it not been for the pig—the name given by all climbers to their haul bags.

Ours was an old green Army surplus duffle bag that I'd repurposed for big-wall climbing by sewing inch-wide webbing around the outside for reinforcement. The pig contained our sleeping bags, water, Campbell's soup, Slim Jims, salami, and bagels—about 50 pounds worth of critical supplies. And it was already slowing us down. I tried lugging it in one arm, then the other. Finally, I put it on like a backpack, threading my arms through the webbing. By the time we reached the base, I had two red welts where the painfully thin straps had sliced into my shoulder joints.

Lesson learned. Sort of. In retrospect, I was just beginning to understand that big-wall climbing is about more than climbing. For starters, it's a multiday backpacking adventure on vertical terrain. Minor inefficiencies, like using a duffle bag instead of an actual haul bag, can become major issues—or at least major inconveniences.

I hadn't thought much about the camping element of the ascent. All my attention had gone into making sure I had the right rack—the collective term for the camming devices, nuts, hexes, slings, and carabiners—required to scale the Nose. Climbers move up the wall by jamming their hands and feet into natural cracks in the rock. As they go, they wedge equipment into the cracks that they clip their rope into to catch them in case they fall.

The Nose can be terrifying because there are long sections where the wall is very smooth and the natural cracks are too tiny to fit even a finger, let alone step a foot. In those cases climbers do what's called aid climbing. They slot a small metal nut into the impossibly thin fissure at a point just above a constriction so the nut can't slip down. The nut is attached to a thick metal cord that they can grab as a handhold and attach an aider—a small ladder made of webbing—to step up on.

Similarly, there are long sections of the Nose where the cracks are too large to fit a hand but too small to get part of the upper body, or a leg, inside. These are known as off-width cracks, and they are considered the most challenging type of crack. For those sections, there is only one piece of gear that will work—a large spring-loaded camming device known as a #4 Friend, created in the 1970s by Yosemite climber Ray Jardine.

It took Mike and me years to accumulate all the specific sizes and types of gear we'd need on the Nose. For college students, climbing equipment can be prohibitively expensive. The #4 Friend was $60 in 1988 (which equates to roughly $122 today). We'd wait for sales at REI to buy hexes, nuts, and carabiners. I also bought some pieces from desperate climbers in Yosemite hocking their gear for gas or lunch money. Mike and I owned three Friends—the most expensive piece on the rack—between the two of us, including one #4, which my dad had gotten me for Christmas. In my mind the worst thing that could happen on the Nose was getting to a section and not having the right gear to send it. What did I know?

It was nearly light out by the time Mike and I reached the base of the Nose, which, in climbing terms, is a southeast-facing buttress. To the layperson, it's a stark gray rock wall that you have to lean your head way back to see. And even then you can't see the top. But we didn't have time to gawk—we had a goal to get to Dolt Tower before anyone else.

I flaked out the rope, making sure it was free from knots and tangles. Mike tied one end into the harness around his waist using a secure knot known as a figure-eight loop. He would lead the "approach," a rocky scramble up to the official start at pitch 1. As the "leader," Mike was in charge of placing the protective gear, or simply "pro," into cracks and clipping in his rope as he ascended in case of a fall. He wore all the equipment that he'd need clipped to the sides of his harness or draped over his shoulder on a sling.

As the "follower," I would stay on the ground while Mike climbed the approach. I was responsible for belaying him. I manipulated the other end of the rope into a belay device and attached it to my harness. The device made it easy for me to feed Mike rope as he climbed, and to lock it off, i.e., keep tension on it, to catch him if he fell. Once Mike reached the top of the approach—a platform about 180 feet up—he would rig an "anchor" to safely attach himself to the wall. Then I'd climb up behind him, retrieving the pro he'd placed as I went.

We planned to trade off leads, or what's known as swinging leads. As for the pig, well, it had a rope all its own and was the leader's responsibility.

Mike tied the pig into its rope using a figure-eight knot, then clipped the other end into his harness. He wouldn't be towing the pig as he climbed—that would be quite a feat. The pig's rope was long enough that Mike could climb to the platform at the top of the approach with the bag still on the ground. Once Mike was secure up there, he'd clip a small pulley to the anchor and thread the pig's rope through it so he could haul the bag up.

Mike and I didn't say much as we made our final checks. It was a comfortable silence, a "let's get 'er done" kind of silence that we'd developed from four years of climbing and running track together in college. I'm sure the magnitude of what we were about to do weighed on both of us, but neither of us wanted to admit that we were intimidated by the Nose. Instead, we were all business—looking each other over to make sure we'd tied our knots correctly and locked our carabiners. Then Mike stepped up onto the wall.

For being the most iconic rock climb on the planet, the Nose has a pretty lackluster approach. It's basically a messy heap of giant rocks. You can technically scramble up it without a rope (which I've done numerous times since that first attempt), but on our first ascent, we were too intimidated by the exposure.

I watched Mike carefully pick his way through the massive rock pile. During his effort I fed a steady stream of rope through the belay device. After about 30 minutes I no longer felt the persistent tug of his upward movement, so I guessed he had finished. Sure enough, a few minutes later Mike called down, "Off belay." That meant he had rigged the anchor and was safely clipped into it.

It was my turn. The follower doesn't actually climb, he "jugs" the rope using handgrips called ascenders, also known as Jumars, after the Swiss inventors who created the device in the late 1950s. I clamped my two ascenders—one per hand—to the rope, which dangled down from the ledge where Mike stood. Then I clipped an aider to the bottom of each ascender to serve as my footholds. For protection, I clipped two pieces of webbing to my harness and attached each to an ascender. This would also enable me to sit back in my harness and take breaks as needed.

Jugging isn't as tough as climbing, but if you get going fast enough, it turns into a decent aerobic workout. And if you rely too much on your arms instead of your legs (or if the wall forces you to because it's over-hung), you can burn out pretty quickly. I wasn't too worried about the physical effort. Given the angle of the approach (which was more a hill than a wall), I'd basically be walking up the line.

Go time. I slid my right-hand ascender up the rope as high as I could reach, gave it a little tug to make sure it had locked on, then stepped up onto the aider. Next I slid the left-hand ascender up to meet its partner and stepped my left foot up. Slide, step, slide, step, slide step . . . I worked my way carefully up the approach.

When I reached the platform, Mike was still struggling to tow the pig. "It's catching on everything down there," he grunted. The pig was designed to be hauled up a vertical wall, and the approach to the Nose is far from vertical. Mike was forced to work way too hard. Still, he had a grin on his face. We were doing it. We were climbing the Nose.

Years later I would learn a way to bypass the inelegant approach by walking around the toe of the buttress to the left and climbing an easy vertical face called Pine Line instead. But on my first attempt, inelegance (and ignorance) was a necessary part of the adventure.

By the time we reached the start of pitch 1, the sun had officially risen over Yosemite Valley. Beyond the forest at the base of El Cap, and beyond the meadow behind it, another granite behemoth called Middle Cathedral Rock was beginning to light up in the sunshine. I studied its silver sheen. The 2,000-foot face shone back, appearing smooth and monochromatic in the sunlight. I noticed the granite at my fingertips looked nothing like it, speckled with crystals in black, white, and silver. The texture wasn't smooth—it was more like a fine sandpaper. The two rocks are made of the same granite. What was different was my vantage point for each.

Mike finally got the pig up to the anchor and promptly chugged water. I joined him. We were still in the shade on our side of the meadow, but I could tell from the early morning temperature that we were in for another 100-degree scorcher by the afternoon.

It was my turn to lead. Pitch 1 is where the actual rock climbing begins—a 130-foot crack climb with ratings of 5.10c and 5.10d. The Yosemite Decimal System is used worldwide and rates climbs from 5.0 to 5.15. Anything 5.10 and higher gets subdivided into a, b, c, and d. Getting into the 5.10-range requires years of training to master, and I was nervous. I planned to get to the top of the pitch any way I could—mostly by aid climbing. On the easiest sections, I'd free-climb, using the natural features of the crack as hand- and footholds, which would be faster because I'd only have to stop and attach gear intermittently for protection. With aid climbing, every move requires inserting gear.

I checked my knot and took a swig of water from the bottle I'd hitched to my harness. Time to climb. The first 10 feet were more of the same scrambling that Mike had endured on the approach. Then it was as if the Nose decided to get serious. The rock heaps smoothed out into a near-vertical wall, with a superhighway of cracks ascending as far as the eye could see. This was the El Capitan we'd been expecting.

I unhooked a piece of pro from my harness and, reaching as high up the wall as I could, carefully slotted it into the crack. Next I unhooked my aider and clipped that into the other end of the pro. Now I had a place to step. I walked up the aider like a ladder, until my waist was even with the pro. From that vantage, I scanned the crack above for my next placement, then pulled another piece of pro off my harness and inserted it. So far, so good. I removed the second aider from my harness and clipped it into the second piece of pro. I gave it a gentle tug to make sure the pro held, then a more aggressive yank. It was solid. I stepped up. As I did so, I reached down to remove the first aider and reattached it to my harness. Finally, I clipped my rope into the second piece of pro and took a deep breath. I would repeat this painstaking sequence about fifteen more times, along with some short stints of free climbing, before I reached the top of pitch 1.

Looking back, I wish I could say I felt great leading my first pitch on the Nose, that it was all very Zen. But I was just plain terrified. Or "gripped," as they say, which somehow sounds cooler. I didn't trust the systems yet. The equipment is more than adequate to keep one 140-pound college grad safely attached to the wall, but that's hard to believe when you're 300 feet off the ground and your life literally depends on it.

I didn't trust myself either. I was a hack with an Army surplus duffle bag instead of a haul bag, and $1.99 gardening gloves with the fingers cut off instead of belay gloves. For the record, it took me almost an hour to climb the 130 feet of pitch 1—a stretch I can do in about 4 minutes today.

By the time I reached the top of pitch 1, indicated by two bolts, I was dripping sweat. I wiped my forehead dry with the back of my glove and went to work setting up an anchor. Climbers build an anchor with a "master point," which is designed to be self-equalized and redundant. I clipped a sling (webbing that can hold up to 5,000 pounds) to each bolt, pulled the slings together to form a V-shape, and then attached a locking carabiner to both slings at the bottom of the V. That locking biner was the master point—the anchor we'd clip ourselves (and the pig) into. If one of the bolts failed, we had a backup because the anchor is rigged off of both.

What if both bolts fail? Highly unlikely. It's not like these were the original bolts that Warren Harding and his team had hammered into the wall. Those first bolts were only a quarter inch in diameter, and while they served their purpose in 1957, they didn't exactly stand the test of time. In the decades following, climbers pulled them out, either intentionally as souvenirs or accidentally because the rusty bolts broke off in their hands. By 1988 organizations like the ASCA (American Safe Climbing Association) had replaced any remaining bolts with larger, sturdier versions and continue to maintain them today.

At the anchor I felt relatively safe. I took a drink of water and got to work towing up the pig. My watch read 9:37 a.m., not quite the speedy start we'd hoped for. Mike jugged up to meet me, clipped into the anchor, and took over the lead for the second pitch. We knew from the climbing-specific topographical map—a detailed diagram of the route—that pitch 2 contained the first pendulum. Pendulums are an exciting feature of big-wall routes, and the Nose has nine of them. Basically a swinging traverse, a pendulum is the simplest way to move laterally, to go from one crack to another.

As I belayed, I watched Mike work his way up the crack. After about 40 minutes and much effort, he came to a bolt that identified the spot to pendulum. He clipped in and yelled down to lower him. I fed rope through the belay device and he slowly descended. "Okay," Mike yelled, after about 10 feet worth, and I locked him off. Hanging in his harness, Mike pushed off the wall with his feet to scoot to the left. He spotted a piton but couldn't quite reach it. So he scooted right to get some momentum and then leapt sideways, running across the wall to the left. This time he got far enough to grab the piton and clipped into it.

"Nice!" I called from below. I was partially jealous and partially relieved that Mike had gotten the first pendulum instead of me. I watched as he scanned the wall for a spot to place his next piece of pro. From below, I couldn't see anything. After a few moments he called down, "This doesn't look good." Then a long pause. I saw him place a small nut below the piton, which is technically the wrong direction to place gear. Then he took another long pause.

"There's nowhere else to go," he said finally. I found that hard to believe. I knew pitch 2 was rated harder than pitch 1 but not by so much that Mike would get stuck. Something must be wrong.

I waited.

"Seriously," he said. I could hear the frustration in his voice. I watched him make an anchor out of the piton and the quarter-inch nut he'd placed below it. Then Mike clipped into the master point and hung suspended in his harness. His shoulders drooped. After a moment he said, "I'm going to need you to come up here."

What? I didn't say the word out loud but yelled it in my head. Climbers don't give up their lead that easily. Something was seriously wrong.

I took Mike off belay, clamped my ascenders onto the rope, and jugged up to where he was hanging. Because we weren't sure if it was possible to leave the pig behind, Mike hauled it as I jugged. Once all three of us were at the anchor, Mike and I switched out the lead so I could investigate. I attached an aider to the anchor and stood up in it to scan the wall above. It looked smooth and slabby, with barely a sliver of a crack running through it. Mike was right, no place to put gear.

I was about to tell him so when it happened: The piton shifted. I slipped, and before I could regain my balance, the piton dislodged completely and I fell backward—stunned, confused, and certain I was about to die.

The rope pulled taut and yanked me to a stop. The small nut Mike had placed under the piton caught me. And him. And the pig. *Holy shit.* We'd been saved by the redundancy of the master point. Mike looked at me with the same face I'm pretty sure I was looking back at him with—eyes bugged, jaw dropped. A quarter-inch nut was all that held the both of us, and our pig, to the wall.

That single nut, its shape probably already deformed from the strain of the fall, could be one granite crystal away from popping out of the fingernail-size crack that Mike had plugged it into.

Adrenaline coursed through me as I grabbed a piece of pro from my harness and slid it into the same small crack. I hurried to clip my rope in. Mike did the same. I exhaled. Then for good measure, I added a third piece of pro and clipped into that too. Now I was triple-protected. "Are you okay?" Mike asked. "Yeah," I said. But I wasn't.

⸻

We needed to find another way up the Nose. We'd either gotten off route, or the given route was too difficult for our skill level. Either way required a do-over on pitch 2. We backtracked to the pendulum point, an act that forced us to leave two pieces of gear behind in the wall—an expensive mistake.

At the pendulum I tried swinging right instead of left. About 10 feet over was the crack—a very climbable crack—that we'd mistakenly thought was to the left. I was shaken from the fall and annoyed with myself for not double-checking the climbing topo before we started pitch 2. A bulbous rock feature had blocked our view of the crack we were supposed to swing over to, which made us automatically assume the crack was the other way. Plus, there'd been that decoy piton. I've since learned that unless you come upon bolts with a known purpose—at the top of the pitch to make an anchor or for a pendulum—a lone piece of gear typically means Wrong Way. It's hard evidence that another climber went there and bailed, much like we had.

I finished out pitch 2, physically anyway. Mentally, I'd lost my confidence and kept double-checking that each piece of gear I placed would hold my weight once I stepped up onto the aider. This slowed me down. It's taken decades of climbing for me to grasp that speed itself is not dangerous, but danger, or more accurately, being scared of danger, slows you down to a miserably inefficient rate. Case in point: By the time I finished pitch 2, the sun had moved across the sky enough that we were no longer in the shade. The rock reflected white-hot sunshine and the rubber in my climbing shoes felt like it was melting into my toes. It was 1 p.m.

Mike took the third pitch. As I belayed, I relaxed enough to realize I was in survival mode—a fight-or-flight kind of autopilot where I was just going through the motions, just trying to make it through. Dolt Tower, at pitch 11, seemed very, very far. I remembered a story about Royal Robbins, another climber from Warren Harding's era, who made a solo ascent of the Muir route on El Capitan, a climb he called his most challenging. He famously said that when he got about two-thirds of the way up, he didn't think he had enough energy (or food or water) to make it to the top. So he decided to do only one more pitch. Then after that pitch, he decided to do just one more. And so on. Robbins reached the top, taking it literally one pitch at a time. I could do the same.

I led the fourth pitch with renewed resolve. But I still struggled with the mental game. Every move I made felt like it came with a 50-50 chance of life or death. Those odds paralyzed me. The pitch seemed to last forever. It felt incredibly unnatural to move so slowly. At the same time, I couldn't seem to speed up. At the top of the pitch, I heaved myself onto Sickle Ledge. A wave of relief flooded my senses—finally, a solid, flat surface. Sickle Ledge was large enough to stand, sit, and even walk a couple steps on.

Six hundred feet below sat El Capitan Meadow, a half-moon-shaped plot of grass with the Merced River snaking around it. The forest we'd hiked through to get to the base looked like broccoli. I went to work hauling the pig as Mike jugged up to the ledge. Once the bag was secure, I realized I was starving and downed a couple bagels and the salami. Then I sat down and closed my eyes. When I opened them, Mike was clamoring over the ledge. "Jesus, it's getting dark already," he said. The sun had moved 180 degrees across the sky.

I ran the numbers in my head. We'd done four pitches, moving at an average rate of 3 hours per pitch. We had six more pitches to climb before we reached Dolt Tower—our original goal for the day—or another 24 hours of straight climbing. That was not going to happen.

Mike looked like he was having the same thought, but neither one of us wanted to say it out loud. Theoretically we could sleep comfortably on Sickle Ledge, but we'd be way behind the next day. "How's the food and water?" I asked. Mike disappeared into the pig and came up with bad news: We'd gone through more than half of our supplies.

I was surprised. We'd consumed half our food and water in 13 hours? I remembered drinking a decent amount of water but didn't remember eating much at all. We had twenty-seven more pitches to go, about another 80 hours of climbing at the current rate. Not only was it not going to happen, it wasn't even possible. A journey of 1,000 miles may begin with a single step, but a journey of 1,000 miles can't happen on 100 miles worth of fuel.

"We're screwed," Mike said, echoing my sentiment.

I nodded. At age 24 I wasn't used to feeling my own mortality so viscerally. I didn't like the way it caught in the back of my throat and made my voice quiver. I knew bailing was the only responsible option—there was nowhere to go but down. We used the rappel bolts that run alongside the lower section of the Nose to descend on our ropes, tails between our legs, back to the forest. Then back to our college town of San Luis Obispo. It would be a year before I returned to the Nose.

CHAPTER 2

Redemption Climb

Crouching under a highway overpass in Los Angeles, I pulled two rocks from a well-worn book bag and carefully coated the flat side of each with PC-7, an epoxy adhesive paste. I stood facing the concrete wall, a rock in each hand, scanning for just the right placement. From overhead, the *woosh, woosh, woosh* of cars speeding past reminded me I was a long way from Yosemite.

I stretched my left arm up overhead and pressed the first rock firmly against the wall, keeping a steady pressure on it as I reached my right arm up and out and pressed the second rock about 3 feet over. I began counting down from sixty in my head to give the adhesive time to dry.

A deep voice bellowed, "Stop right there."

I whipped my head around to see two police officers hurrying toward me, their hands on their holsters. "We got a call about graffiti," said Officer no. 1 gruffly. "Stay where you are and put your hands in the air."

My hands were already in the air.

"What exactly are you doing?" asked Officer no. 2.

I explained that I was a rock climber. I nodded my head toward the book bag full of rocks at my feet. The officers' expressions turned from stern to curious. I let go of the handholds. "When I'm done, it will be a traverse," I said. "It will span this entire wall."

The policemen smiled. Officer no. 1 pinched one of the holds with his fingertips and gave it a little tug. Luckily, it held. "This is good work you're doing here, man," he said. And they turned and left.

Admittedly, Los Angeles wasn't the best place for a 25-year-old guy who loved to climb. But I needed a job, and shortly before bailing on the Nose with Mike in July, I'd interviewed for a position as production manager at a manufacturer called Parker Seals in LA and gotten it. I'd moved to the cement jungle not long after returning from Yosemite.

My parents were elated. It had taken me six years to earn my economics degree, mostly due to the distraction of climbing. I'm pretty sure they thought I was going to end up a climbing bum. Instead, I was a yuppie. Or a yuppie-in-training, anyway, earning a steady paycheck in the big city, living in a modest yet respectable one-bedroom apartment.

Rock-climbing gyms didn't yet exist in California in 1989, so in the city, climbers made their own beneath LA's insufferable tangle of roadways. Every Tuesday and Thursday after work, I did laps on the wall closest to my apartment—an 80-foot-long traverse that covered both sides of a concrete column beneath Overland Avenue. A handful of other climbers trained there, mostly dudes, and most with a Walkman attached to the waistband of their shorts. This was the extent of my social life in LA.

On weekends I drove 2 hours to Joshua Tree National Park to climb. Now that I was living in LA, Joshua Tree was a lot closer than Yosemite. Most of the time, Mike met me at Joshua Tree. After graduation (and our failed Nose climb), he'd moved to San Diego for an engineering job. In Joshua Tree we didn't speak of the Nose. Maybe we both just wanted to forget about it. Or maybe life was moving forward too quickly. We both had real jobs, had recently moved to new cities, and were trying on our adult lives. Mike even had a girlfriend. Meanwhile, I discovered a different kind of love interest: climbing competitions.

"Rock 'til You Drop" the flyer read. Sport Chalet, a retailer just north of LA, was hosting California's first climbing competition. The news spread fast—in the late 1980s, climbing comps were big in Europe but a novel concept in the United States. The only one I'd been to was the Phoenix Bouldering Contest, held on natural rock at Oak Flat Campground in Arizona. Sport Chalet's competition would be different, held on an artificial wall like the high-end European events. Every climber I knew in SoCal was planning to be there.

I showed up at Sport Chalet on the day of the competition, a warm, sunny morning in May. The parking lot had been converted into a festival of sorts, with booths and vendors, and a "Welcome Summer" sale in full swing. I found the Climbing Comp booth and registered, and was sent to "Isolation," an area around the corner and out of sight of the climbing wall. The idea was to prevent competitors from gaining an unfair advantage by watching (and learning from) the mistakes of preceding climbers.

In the isolation corner rumors flew about the wall. "It's like 50 feet high," said one young climber. "There's an overhang," said a stocky guy in cut-off jean shorts. "The belayers don't know what they're doing—someone got dropped," said a ponytailed woman. While we couldn't see the wall, we could see the spectators and gauge how well a climb was going by the audience's reaction. Cheers and applause meant success, collective groans meant falls.

When my name was called, I walked around the corner to the competition wall. A row of judges sat in metal folding chairs facing the redbrick wall. Three routes, each indicated by a dangling toprope, awaited. The one on the far right was for round 1. Climbers who made it to the top would progress to round 2 and a more difficult route.

I tied into the rope and shook hands with my belayer, an older guy in shorts and no shirt. He looked competent enough. I looked up at the route. It was my first glimpse of synthetic climbing holds, equipment that would one day be commonplace in climbing gyms all across the United States. Each hand- and foothold was gray in color and attached to the brick wall by a bolt through the center. The route ascended the brick wall to the building's roof, then continued up a 20-foot sheet of plywood that Sport Chalet had erected on top of the roof.

I reached up and grasped the first hold, stepping my feet onto the smaller holds close to the ground. I worked my way up the wall, grasping the larger holds with my hands, and standing on whatever I could find for the feet. I made it to the top with energy to spare.

My reward was a trip back around the corner to Isolation to wait for round 2. It was there that I started to get a sense for the scope of the competition. I found out that Mari Gingery, the queen of the Joshua Tree climbing scene, was there. She'd been racking up first ascents since the late 1970s, and in 1988 she'd nabbed the FA of Elephant Rock, which had an impressive rating (for that time period) of 5.11d. Bill Leventhal was also there, a SoCal climbing legend in his own time, responsible for pushing the difficulty on all the local crags by making a slew of FAs that went way beyond 5.10.

When it was my turn again, the judges instructed me to climb the center rope. The start was similar to the first route—gray holds on red brick—but the route setters had added a piece of plywood near the top of the brick, changing the orientation of the wall from vertical to mildly overhanging. Then, at the point where the brick wall ended and the plywood wall on the roof began, they'd added a second piece of plywood at the opposite angle to make a slab. Finally, at the very top, they'd bolted an aggressively overhanging piece of plywood. The fact that the plywood additions were painted black, with neon swirls in hot pink, lime green, and yellow, gave a clear 1980s-style message: This is going to be rad.

By then a crowd had gathered. It seemed more people came to watch the climbing competition than to shop at the sale. When I made it past the overhang, people actually cheered. I didn't know it at the time, but I was one of only two men who'd managed to climb the feature without falling.

For the finals, round 3, I waited in Isolation while my competition, Bill Leventhal, climbed. I could tell by the cheers that he'd had a successful bid. When it was my turn, the first thing I noticed was that the route looked really similar to round 2, but instead of an aggressive overhang at the very top, there was a *really* aggressive overhang, so much so that it was technically considered a roof—the climbing term for an overhang that's so severe it makes a nearly 90-degree angle with the wall. *Here goes nothing*, I thought.

I don't know if it was adrenaline or habit from competing in track and field in college, but I started fast. Really fast. And never slowed down. Even at the roof, a natural pause point, my brain reminded my body, *you're safe, you're on a toprope*, and I just hurled myself over it. The crowd ate it up, and I reached the top to enthusiastic applause and a few whoops and hollers.

The judges were now faced with a tie situation since Bill and I had both successfully climbed all three routes. They gathered together and spoke quietly for a few minutes. Then one stepped forward and declared me the winner because I'd "climbed it the fastest."

Winning California's first-ever climbing competition wasn't as important to me as climbing the Nose had been. But the success felt gratifying or at least offered some encouragement that I wasn't a total hack. I started researching climbing competitions and found out that the same weekend I won in May, England had hosted the first World Cup contest in the history of climbing. Thousands of people showed up to watch the inaugural event, which was televised all over the world.

Four more World Cup climbing competitions were scheduled in Europe for the summer and fall, and one was scheduled for the United States—in Snowbird, Utah—in August. Meanwhile, an American alpinist and entrepreneur named Jeff Lowe had created a national climbing series that would kick off in August, also at Snowbird, the weekend before the World Cup.

It was like a new chapter in the book of rock climbing was being written. And I was intrigued. Could people actually earn a living by rock climbing? I decided to test my mettle at Jeff Lowe's national series, starting in Snowbird on August 11, 1989. To compete, I'd need to mail a written application detailing my qualifications to the sport-climbing committee of the American Alpine Club. Luckily, I had the win at Sport Chalet under my belt.

When my acceptance letter arrived, I felt kind of like I'd qualified for the Olympics. I found myself climbing with new zeal on the "glue-ups" under the highways. I also found myself thinking about the Nose. Yosemite was back on the table for weekends, mostly by default—it was too hot to climb in Joshua Tree in the summer, when temperatures soared over 110°F. I called up Mike and asked if he wanted to meet me in Yosemite the following weekend.

At work I caught myself replaying the Nose climb in my head, analyzing it like I was looking for inefficiencies in a production line. I realized how much the fall after the first pendulum had spooked me, when the piton had dislodged, and how much I'd let fear hold me back after that. But at the same time, I wasn't sure what I could have done differently. The fear was legit. Wasn't it?

On the drive to Yosemite, my mind went round and round on the question of fear, looking for a specific reason why the climb had been a failure. Finally, I decided there was no single answer. For a variety of reasons, the climb hadn't worked out. Kind of like my last couple of dates. I turned up the music to stop thinking.

When I got to Yosemite, I found myself avoiding the Nose and all the big-wall climbs in Yosemite Valley, like the way you steer clear of your ex-girlfriend and her friends at social events. Instead, Mike and I climbed in Tuolumne Meadows—an area on the east side of the park that's known for short- to medium-length routes. We worked our way through the 5.10-rated climbs and even some of the 5.11s. It was a great workout and a great weekend. But it wasn't exactly closure on the Nose.

In the days that followed, I even started dreaming about the Nose. I'd wake up feeling antsy, like I needed to do something, anything. So I'd go for a really fast run. Or plan a marathon climbing session after work, preloading my Walkman with a favorite cassette tape so I could zone out and traverse for hours.

The next time Mike and I met in Yosemite, two weekends later, I casually mentioned that I had the Nose on the brain. Mike told me he'd been thinking about it too. He said he wanted to get married to his girlfriend and felt like sending the Nose was something he needed to do before he could settle down. "It's like I need to get it out of my system," he said. I understood. Sort of. I wasn't entirely sure why I was suddenly fixated on the Nose again.

Before driving back to LA, I went to El Capitan Meadow and sat in the grass. It was a place I knew well—a popular gathering spot where climbers bask in the sun, cool off in the Merced River, and trade beta (intelligence) about big-wall climbing. It's also the best view of El Cap from anywhere in the valley. The massive cliff is only about a half-mile away, just far enough to be able to see all of it, end to end, top to bottom, all in one plane.

From that vantage point, El Cap is at its most mesmerizing. The granite rises up from the evergreens like a gigantic movie screen. And people treat it as such, setting up chairs and throwing down picnic blankets in the open field to watch. At first it's impossible to spot climbers—they're like ants on the wall. But with a bit of concentration, you can train your eyes to see them. Your mind says no, that can't be real, those can't be humans up there. But it is, they are.

I sat and studied the Nose, admiring the way it juts out, almost belligerently, at the juncture of the southwest and southeast faces. In the waning afternoon light, I watched the color of the granite shift from shimmering silver to concrete gray. It occurred to me that next weekend was the Fourth of July, the same weekend that Mike and I had failed on the Nose the previous year. As the sun started to set, I began to understand that I couldn't go to Snowbird to compete at nationals with unfinished business in Yosemite. Call it ego, call it compulsion, call it the naivety of youth, but it was like having a black mark on my permanent record. Never mind the fact that people on the competition circuit didn't care who had climbed the Nose and who hadn't. I couldn't step into the world of competitive rock climbing as a Yosemite hack.

By the time I'd driven home, I'd made my decision. I called up Mike, "So I've got an idea for what we could do for your bachelor party. . . ."

In July 1989 in Yosemite Valley, temperatures hovered around 100°F for the second summer in a row, with no sign of relief. And it was crowded. Now that I was part of the working class, I hadn't been able to get there early enough to secure a campsite on a holiday weekend. It was 5:30 p.m. and everything was taken. Mike was undaunted. "Let's just start," he said.

Well that would solve the problem of where to legally sleep—we'd be on the wall. And the temperature was certainly more manageable at that time of day. Mike may have been joking, but I liked the idea.

Thirty minutes later we'd sorted our gear and were hiking to the base of El Capitan. I felt surprisingly relaxed. Perhaps because this climb already felt markedly different from the first, based on what time of day we were starting. Or maybe I had more confidence because I knew what to expect. Either way, those first four pitches went smoothly. We moved efficiently, even quickly. When we started to lose light, we donned our headlamps and kept climbing. We made it to Sickle Ledge—the place where we aborted the prior year's attempt—moments before the sky went completely black.

As we sat on the ledge eating a late dinner of bagels and beef jerky by headlamp, I marveled that it had taken us more than 12 hours to reach Sickle Ledge the year before. This time, it had taken us three. Mike's response, between mouthfuls: "What's amazing is the way you track that stuff. Are you sure it wasn't, like, 3 hours and 8 minutes?" (Actually, it was more like 3 hours and 19 minutes. But I was happy to round down.)

Later in my climbing career, I learned that the first four pitches of the Nose are not representative of the rest of the climb. Not only are they technically challenging, lacking solid cracks for gear placement, but the hauling is abnormally difficult. The pig is at its heaviest, and you're yanking it up a low-angle slab instead of a flat vertical wall. After the first four pitches, the Nose only gets better.

We slept well after dinner. Sickle Ledge is large enough to fit two guys and a pig, and then some. Though it was dark, I could tell that the route had moved slightly off the prow to the right, which made the ledge feel tucked in and protected. To be extra safe, both Mike and I had attached ourselves to the wall by connecting our harnesses to an anchor using a couple lengths of webbing.

We didn't sleep long—more like a nap. I was wide awake at 1 a.m. and thinking about night climbing. It seemed like a smart way to beat the heat. We could get a super-early start and then nap in a shady spot when the sun was at its peak. It wasn't how people typically climbed the Nose, but it made sense. At least in theory.

Mike wasn't too hard to convince. Like me, he had to be back at work on Tuesday, so time was of the essence. We donned our headlamps and tied into the rope. Mike took the first lead. Pretty much as soon as he was a few feet overhead, he was out of reach of my headlamp beam. Fortunately, belaying happens mostly by feel, not sight. I switched off my headlamp to save battery and was immediately engulfed in the black of a new moon.

As Mike climbed pitch 5, I fed a steady stream of rope, being extra careful not to leave too much slack in the line in case he fell. As my eyes adjusted, the stars came out in full force. I turned away from the wall to face the open void. There were thousands and thousands of stars and no moonlight to drown them out. I felt like I was bearing witness to something that very few human eyes had seen before.

"Off belay!" Mike called down. He'd made quick work of the pitch. I switched my headlamp back on and changed out my belay device for ascenders. Meanwhile, I heard the pig begin its hairy ascent, scraping against the wall as Mike towed it from above. Time to jug. After a few minutes I realized why Mike had moved so fast—the entire pitch was Class 4, or in layman's terms, easy. If we hadn't been 700 feet above ground, in the dark, I could have walked up it, like a steep, rocky staircase.

What wasn't easy was hauling the pig up nonvertical terrain. Mike was still fighting with it when I reached the top of the pitch. I let him utter a few more curse words before I offered to take over hauling. He refused. It was apparently a battle he needed to win on his own.

So I went to work anchoring in and setting up to lead the next pitch. Once Mike was done cursing and had me on belay, I started to climb. The beam from my headlamp reduced pitch 6 to a bubble of light about 5 feet in diameter. I followed a rocky, left-facing corner, aid climbing in my bubble, unable to see anything beyond except for the occasional microscopic headlight beam from a car driving past El Capitan Meadow.

People mistakenly assume that climbing by headlamp is less intimidating because you can't tell how high you are, but you feel the exposure in other ways. I was very aware of the blackness that surrounded me; all that empty space enveloping me, pushing in on me, threatening to extinguish me—an existential kind of terror.

Mike and I climbed through the inky darkness like big-wall ninjas to reach the Stove Leg crack, which spans pitches 8, 9, and 10. I knew the Stove Legs as the part of the climb that had stumped Warren Harding and his team for weeks during the first ascent. At the time, there were no pitons, the protection used in 1957, wide enough to insert into the crack, which gets as wide as 4 inches in places and runs straight up the center of El Cap's prow for a good 400 feet.

The way the story goes, Harding's buddy Frank Traver found an old wood-burning stove with iron legs at the Berkeley dump. He brought the legs to Yosemite, and Harding promptly took them up the wall, pounding them into the crack like a ladder. He moved up the ladder by pounding out the lowest stove leg and "leapfrogging" it to the top. Thus he conquered the crack, and the Stove Legs got their name.

It was my turn to lead the first section of the Stove Legs, a steady 2-inch-wide crack. I started up it using a free-climbing technique called hand jamming. First I turned my right hand sideways, with the thumb facing up, and slid it into the crack. Then I drew my thumb across my palm to expand my hand, so that I couldn't pull it back out. I did the same with my left hand, slotting it into the crack a bit higher. I knew from muscle memory achieved during years of climbing that a hand jam is nearly as strong as a ladder rung. Still, I felt nervous as I stepped one foot into the crack and stood up on it. The hand jams held. I put my other foot into the crack above the first foot. When I was sure I was stable, I released my right hand and slid it out of the crack, reinserting it above the left. I did the same with the left hand, reinserting it above the right. Then I stepped one foot up, followed by the other.

After about 10 feet of hand jamming my way up the crack, I knew I needed to put in a piece of pro. I released my right hand to pull a #2.5 Friend—a camming device that fits in cracks no more than 2.5 inches wide—off my climbing harness and slid it into the crack at waist height. Then I clipped in my rope. I hand-jammed my way up another 10 feet and inserted a second #2.5 Friend. I was about to start hand jamming again when it hit me—I was going to run out of gear.

While I couldn't see the upper reaches of the crack in the dark, I knew from the climbing topo that it extended all the way up the pitch, about another 70 feet worth. And I had no more #2.5 Friends left. I had plenty of the less expensive nuts and hexes, as well as a #3 and #4 Friend, but nothing that fit the crack. I suddenly understood how Warren Harding must have felt.

"Take!" I yelled down to Mike in the darkness. He took in the slack in the rope.

"I need to lower. Give me about 10 feet," I called out.

Mike obliged, and I lowered down the wall back to my first #2.5 Friend and pulled it out. As much as I hated having to go down in order to go up, I didn't see any other way to do it. Mike understood what was happening and helped get me back up to my second #2.5 Friend by counterweighting the rope from his end. I continued climbing, hand jamming my way above the second #2.5 Friend, and then placed my retrieved #2.5 Friend above it.

I knew I couldn't go on like that. Not only was it time-consuming (and energy-sapping) to go back and forth shuttling my pro, it was also dangerous to be hanging off just one piece of gear while Mike lowered me down. As I was puzzling over my predicament, I hand-jammed up a bit farther, hoping the crack widened enough to fit my #3 Friend. Lo and behold, it did. In a moment of sheer dumb luck, I now had three pieces of gear to work with.

I left the lowest #2.5 where it was, as my fail-safe in case of a fall. Then I continued climbing Stove Legs by leapfrogging my second #2.5 with my #3. I'd plug one piece at waist height, climb above it, and place the second piece, then reach back and pull out the first. It wasn't fast, but it was safe. I spent just over an hour on pitch 8, which increased to 1.5 hours once Mike jugged up to meet me and I'd hauled up the pig. Unfortunately, we still had two more pitches worth of the Stove Legs to climb.

By the time we reached Dolt Tower, just after the Stove Legs, the sun had risen. Another party was just waking up on the ledge. They were shocked to see us come clamoring over the edge. "Good morning!" I bellowed. I should have been exhausted, but I was amped. Something about the daylight completely reinvigorated me. We shimmied around the groggy climbers to the far side of the modest ledge, where piles of rocks make it impossible to lay down, but they provide a decent place to sit.

Mike and I ate breakfast perched on the Dolt Tower ledge, some 1,200 feet above the valley floor, staring out across El Cap Meadow to the granite peaks and spires of Cathedral Rocks. I checked the climbing topo and cracked a joke about the fact that we'd come so far and yet were only about one-third of the way up the Nose. We had three more pitches—relatively easy compared to Stove Legs—to El Cap Tower, the largest ledge on the route. There would be more room on El Cap Tower to lay down and nap, so we agreed to keep moving.

Mike lowered me off Dolt Tower to the right, to a corner with a slot—climber-speak for a deep, narrow chimney—that marks the start of pitch 12. Ascending the slot felt a bit awkward, and I was glad when it gave way to a pair of thin hand cracks. Compared to the Stove Legs, it felt like we flew up the next couple pitches. We made it to El Cap Tower, located at the base of pitch 15, in less than 2 hours.

The smooth gray ledge looked incredibly comfortable—nice and flat, about the width of single bed and three times as long. There was plenty of room to sleep. But the last thing I wanted to do was close my eyes—the view had reached epic proportions. Looking to either side, I could see straight down Yosemite Valley, an infinity of miniature forests lined with towering gray granite. Gazing straight ahead across El Cap Meadow, I could see *over* the Cathedral Rock formations to the southern rim of Yosemite.

I turned to Mike. "We're about to get to the really good stuff—Texas Flake, Boot Flake, the Great Roof. I want to see them in daylight. We can't sleep now."

Mike agreed and took the first pitch off El Cap Tower to get us up to Texas Flake. Standing on top of the large sheet of rock, whose shape calls to mind the Lone Star State, and looking up at Boot Flake, I decided the word "flake" didn't do these features justice. From El Cap Meadow you can see both of them with the naked eye. Up close, they are mind-blowing, appearing to float on the wall with no connection whatsoever. From what I could tell, Boot Flake was less than 2 feet thick.

I've since learned that "flake" is a geologic term and that the Nose's flakes are a product of a natural process known as exfoliation. What geologists aren't exactly sure about is why El Capitan sheds sheets of rock in the first place. One theory is that it releases the pressure that builds up from, say, temperature shifts and tectonic uplift. Like a concrete driveway where laborers cut preemptive fissures when the concrete is poured so that it will crack there later, rocks in the wild relieve their stress along preexisting fissures. El Capitan has very few natural cracks and fissures, so it exfoliates.

I'd heard, through climbing lore, that the Nose's flakes could theoretically peel off the wall at any point. I've since learned that fact is not an exaggeration. As one Yosemite park ranger told me, it's not a question of *if* Texas Flake and Boot Flake will fall off El Capitan but rather *when*.

But that first time, I started climbing from Texas Flake to Boot Flake blissfully unaware of the extent of the risk. My focus was on navigating the "bolt ladder." The wall between the two flakes is blank, with no place to wedge even the tiniest piece of pro, so it's permanently bolted—a 50-foot-long "ladder" of predrilled bolts forms a diagonal line from the top left corner of Texas Flake to the natural crack just below the "heel" of Boot Flake.

Reaching up, I clipped my aider into the first bolt. Then I stepped up onto it and clipped my rope in for protection. I continued that way, moving carefully between bolts using my two aiders. I thought of Warren Harding, who had to create his own bolt ladder on the first ascent by drilling holes straight into the rock face and then hammering in bolts. It must have been an arduous process.

I moved carefully, clipping and unclipping, clipping and unclipping. About halfway through, I realized I was holding my breath. I exhaled. I noticed my next inhale was jagged and shaky. I worried I was bonking and stopped. But I didn't feel exhausted. In fact, I didn't want to stop, I wanted to get through the rest of the bolt ladder as quickly as possible. That's when it hit me: I was gripped.

There I was, some 1,500 feet above the ground, relying on a few measly bolts to keep me from plummeting to certain death. The "granite sea" between Texas Flake and Boot Flake drops straight to the ground, with no ledges to break your fall or even a nearby crack to grab for. The exposure made everything else on the route seem suddenly tame in comparison.

Even the shape of the wall at this point on the route is nerve-racking. Instead of stretching reliably behind me in both directions, it disappeared around a corner to expose more open sky—a subconscious reminder of how vulnerable I was up there, clinging to a tiny bolt on a mammoth rock face.

As my mind analyzed the fear, I came to understand that I was in uncharted Nose terrain. Perhaps I'd gotten a little too comfortable with the style of the first fifteen pitches and was having a wake-up call of sorts; a reminder that this is difficult and scary. I worked to steady my breathing. Eventually—I knew this from previous experience—my mind would adapt, and the fear would not be so acute.

"You okay?" Mike asked from his belay perch on Texas Flake.

"Yeah," I said, and I meant it.

I started to climb again. Although I didn't fully process it at the time, I'd learned an important lesson on the bolt ladder: Climbing isn't about being fearless, it's about how you manage that fear. For me, it helps to understand its source. I still felt gripped as I moved from one bolt to the next, but I knew why, and that knowledge kept me from panicking or freezing up.

It's kind of funny, but when I reached the heel of Boot Flake, I felt a wave of relief. I was about to ascend a loosely connected 2-foot-thick sheet of rock that could tear off the wall at any moment and, somehow, it felt "safer" than aid-climbing bolts strung across a sheer rock face. And that's another interesting thing about fear: It's not always rational, and it varies by person. Mike would tell me later that he found climbing on flakes terrifying.

34

Thirty minutes later I'd aid-climbed the 60 or so feet up the heel and calf to the top of Boot Flake. I felt pretty good standing up there, an on-top-of-the-world, I-conquered-my-fear kind of moment. I checked the time: nearly noon. Not bad. I was dripping sweat and drank the rest of my water bottle while Mike jugged up to meet me.

I towed the pig and refilled both our water bottles from the stash inside. "You should get to do the King Swing," Mike said when he got to the anchor. "You did all the work to get to the top of the boot."

I couldn't argue with that. The King Swing is one of the most storied moves in all of climbing—a 100-foot pendulum swing to the left. I was giddy to be the one to do it. From the anchor at the top of Boot Flake, Mike lowered me all the way down to the other side of the boot, past the toe.

"What do you think?" he called down.

"Looks like I need to be a little lower," I said, eyeballing the end of the bolt ladder, which was now on my right, and the gauge for the proper starting point for the swing.

Mike lowered me another couple feet.

"Okay!" I called up, and he jerked me to a stop.

I took a last glance at Mike, who gave me a thumbs-up. I took a deep breath, then jogged over to the right for momentum and then ran left, swinging as far as I could before grabbing the wall with my hands, bracing my feet, and side-crawling the rest of the way to reach Eagle Ledge.

"That was incredible!" Mike yelled.

It really was. In that moment I felt like I could do anything.

Next up was the Grey Bands traverse, pitches 17 through 21. The Grey Bands get their name from the color of the granite, which contains more of the darker minerals, mainly biotite and hornblende, than the rest of the Nose. You can see the Grey Bands from El Cap Meadow. They look like horizontal stripes.

We quickly figured out that the granite of the Grey Bands is not as strong as the rest of the Nose, which results in a lot of fractured rock. On my lead I didn't feel like I was rock climbing so much as hiking, and occasionally crawling, up a steep, crumbly catwalk. The pig, as usual, complicated matters. A person could creep through the Grey Bands, but a 50-pound haul bag, not so much. We had to rig horizontal lines of rope along the face for protection and lug the pig like a backpack, taking it off frequently to hang it from the rope and shove it around a steep corner. We sweated, grunted, and swore our way through the Grey Bands.

By the time we reached pitch 22, which leads up and around the Great Roof, we were starting to lose light. For the first time, I felt exhausted. And hungry. So much that I lacked the appropriate amount of enthusiasm for the Nose's iconic "roof"—a 15-foot overhang that geologists speculate was carved out by a massive rockfall.

Instead of admiring the feature, I cursed it. It was just another roadblock to making it to Camp V—the ledge just above pitch 24—for dinner and sleep. I remembered the horror stories I'd heard about the crack leading up to the Great Roof. Most cracks on the Nose are perfect splitter cracks, which have a slight diagonal orientation that serves to stabilize the gear you place. Not this one—it runs straight up the wall, requiring super-careful placement so the protection doesn't just pull straight down and out. To add insult to injury, it's a painfully thin crack.

At least I didn't have to lead it, I thought. It was Mike's turn. But my belay experience was far from soothing. Mike moved painfully slow in order to make sure his gear was tight in the dicey crack. It took him twice as long as any previous pitch. About halfway through the belay, I was horrified to realize I was fighting to keep my eyes open. Back then, we didn't have Grigris, the belay devices that auto-lock when a climber falls. If Mike fell while I was asleep, there'd be nothing to keep the rope from pulling through and dropping him for a very long fall, likely to his death.

By the time we reached Camp V, it was dark. I was shattered, physically and mentally. Once we'd secured the gear, I went straight to sleep. What time was it? What day was it? I didn't know. I didn't care.

Mike woke me up in the predawn twilight so we could begin climbing as soon at it was light. My head was pounding like a bad hangover. We didn't have much water left, but I was too thirsty to ration and drank my fill. I fished a bagel and the rest of the cheese from the haul bag, and checked the topo as we ate. We had seven pitches to go. If the rest of the climb went as planned, we'd reach the top in about 8 hours—the span of a typical workday. We could do this.

I glanced at the ledge to make sure we hadn't left anything behind, tied into the rope, checked that Mike had me on belay, and made sure I'd attached the pig's rope to my harness. Check, check, check, check. Go time. I looked up and studied the route. I took a breath. I looked up again. I took a swig of water. I looked up again. I looked down at my feet. I wasn't sure I could do this.

After a long pause I turned to Mike. "Can you take this one?" I asked sheepishly.

"You okay?" Mike responded.

"I think so. My head is just really foggy."

We switched out the lead, and Mike took the next two pitches. We rested at the top of pitch 26, on the ledge known as Camp VI. I dozed for a bit, then we ate the rest of our food and finished off the water. My head started to clear. I didn't know it at the time, but pitch 25 is the most accident-prone section of the Nose. The protection is thin and a fall most certainly results in a crash on a lower ledge. Years later I'd help rescue a Korean climber who'd done exactly that, breaking several ribs and an ankle in the process. In 2003 I'd take a fall of my own on pitch 25, slamming my face into the rock and needing my partner, Scott Bovard, to finish the climb.

All I knew that groggy morning in 1989 was that I didn't feel good enough to climb. Luckily, I had a teammate who did. And luckily, I had enough experience playing team sports that I felt gratitude, not shame, in turning over the lead. Looking back, the decision demonstrated a wisdom well beyond my then twenty-five years. Knowing when to say when is perhaps the most important skill you can learn in big-wall climbing. Or the one that keeps you alive the longest, anyway.

I took back the lead for pitch 27. Now that my mind had cleared, I noticed that the Nose's upper dihedral is yet another new type of terrain. After all the exposure of the prior sections, I felt almost claustrophobic. I couldn't see anything from side to side—we were literally climbing up the inside of a corner. Only the view straight across to Cathedral indicated how high we were—the towers and spires of Cathedral Rocks were starting to look small. Nor could I see the top, as a giant overhanging headwall blocked our view.

Looking back, I have almost no memories of those last few pitches. We were in zombie climbing mode. Words were kept to a minimum, like "Your turn," "Good job," and "On belay."

I know I took the final pitch to the top. I vaguely recall the bolt ladder on the overhang being less mentally taxing than the one on the granite sea between the flakes, but far more physically stressful. When Warren Harding made the first ascent, he spent 14 hours on this section, pounding fifteen pitons and twenty-eight bolts.

When I reached the lip that marked the end of the overhang, I heaved myself up onto the final slab and slogged up the final 30 feet to reach the wide-open granite plateau marking the top of El Capitan. As Mike jugged up to meet me, I fished around for my watch. It was Sunday, 4:12 p.m. We'd been on the Nose for approximately 46 hours.

Once Mike and the pig were safely at the top, I stretched out flat on my back and stared up at the sky. It seemed more fitting than looking down at where we'd come from. In that moment I felt like I had more in common with the heavens than with the earth.

I let my eyelids close, reveling in the deep satisfaction that comes from just the right combination of accomplishment and exhaustion. I drifted in and out of sleep, dreaming vivid dreams of granite and open sky and trees so far below that they looked like broccoli. But not in my wildest dreams could I have imagined that by the end of the millennium, I would top out on the Nose another thirty-one times—or why.

CHAPTER 3

Hollywood Hans

Five weeks after sending the Nose for the first time, I flew to Salt Lake City, rented a car, and drove into the Wasatch Mountains to Snowbird for the North American Open. Seventy of the nation's top male and female climbers had descended on the ski town, where we were treated to special discounted lodging and hosted parties. The competition wall stood 115 feet tall and had been built on the outside of a luxury hotel.

The glitzy scene was unlike anything I'd experienced climbing in Yosemite or Joshua Tree, both of which suddenly felt galaxies away. A new era was dawning, or at least a new style of rock climbing was emerging, a variation called "sport" climbing. The type of climbing I was used to doing became known as "traditional" climbing, or trad.

Terming the new breed of climbing "sport" represented a philosophy shift, a movement away from the activity's mountaineering roots, where risk and danger were an integral part of the experience. In sport climbing, whether on a man-made wall like at Snowbird or outdoors on a natural rock face, the route is set by the aptly named route setter, a rock architect of sorts who chooses the line the climb will follow and drills permanent bolts into the wall, about every 10 feet or so, for subsequent climbers to clip their rope into for protection.

Thus, sport climbers no longer needed to carry nuts, hexes, and camming devices to wedge into cracks for protection on their way up a wall. Instead they carry quickdraws, lightweight pieces of equipment consisting of a strip of sewn webbing strung between two carabiners—one to clip into the bolt and the other to thread the rope through. Climbing a bolted sport route takes all the guesswork and fumbling out of placing protection. It's also significantly safer.

That doesn't mean that sport climbing is easy. With much of the risk removed, sport climbers are free to focus on gymnastic-like difficulty, performing incredible feats of strength, balance, and flexibility to ascend routes. New skills like "reading a route," the act of envisioning how the route setter intended each move be made in between the bolts, came into the fold, as did the idea of climbing with style and grace. Sport climbing also helped advance free climbing. With bolted routes, a climber was much safer to practice moves using the natural features of the rock. Aid climbing was suddenly old-school.

I'd been doing sport climbing without really realizing it, in places like Mount Woodson in San Diego. My climbing friends and I knew it as "cragging," or climbing single-pitch (no more than one rope length) bolted routes. I can't say I liked it better or worse than trad climbing. To me, climbing was climbing, and I liked it all.

The North American Open was all about sport climbing, which was quickly becoming the sexier, more commercialized version of the two. But in the United States at least, the line between sport and trad climbers hadn't been clearly drawn yet, so Snowbird drew both types. Looking around, I saw sport climbers clad in Lycra tights and tank tops, like Dan Goodwin, who was famous for his televised stunts scaling hundred-floor buildings, as well as Yosemite heroes like Ron Kauk, who'd been climbing in cut-off jean shorts since the 1970s.

Had I been aware of the politics of climbing at the time, I may have picked up on the undercurrent of tension steadily building between old-school climbers and the new, flashier breed of sport climbers. The American Alpine Club had attempted to address the issue three years prior, in 1986, at its annual meeting in Denver, Colorado. On the subject of "climbing ethics," notable old-school Yosemite climbers like Yvon Chouinard and John Bachar spoke out against "rap bolting," the practice of setting sport-climbing routes by hanging from a rappel line.

The technique was already popular in Europe, where sport climbing was en vogue. In the United States it was causing an uproar in Oregon, where a young upstart named Alan Watts was rap bolting new routes at Smith Rock. Chouinard and Bachar, along with Ron Kauk and Dave Robinson, represented the point of view that if you're going to bolt a route, at least do it by climbing from the ground up, placing your own protection as you go. Using a rappel line was perceived as a type of cheating.

Proponents of rap bolting, including Watts, Todd Skinner, and Christian Griffith, argued that it was essential for elite climbers to advance their skill. Not many people could bolt a 5.13 route from the ground up. But by doing it from the top down on rappel, setting 5.13 and greater routes was suddenly very possible. Their ultimate argument was that rap bolting enabled more challenging routes to be more safely created—a win-win for the sport.

The old-school squad also criticized "hangdogging," the practice of dangling from the wall in your harness after a fall, or right before a complicated section, in order to rest or work through the sequence in your head before trying it on the route. At that time the rules in sport climbing were such that a climber who fell must lower back down to the ground and start over. Hangdoggers were "cheating" by resuming the climb from the point where they fell.

At age 25, none of this mattered much to me. My hero at the time was Steve Schneider, a dynamic climber who did it all, and did it all exceptionally well. Schneider was born and raised in Oakland, California, with sun-kissed blond hair and a perpetual tan. He showed up in Yosemite in the spring of 1981 at the age of 21, while on break from Chico State, and never went back.

By 1983 Schneider was holding his own on pretty much any climb in Yosemite, and he nabbed the second ascent of Bachar-Yerian, a heinous 400-foot test piece in Tuolumne Meadows rated 5.11c. In 1984 he was chosen for a coveted position on Yosemite's search and rescue team (SAR). In 1989 he completed the first solo one-day ascent of the Nose. It took him 21 hours and 22 minutes. Climbing a route solo means you have to belay yourself as you aid-climb up, and then rappel down each pitch to clean your gear before jugging back up the rappel line. So Schneider technically climbed the Nose twice (and rappelled it once) in less than 22 hours, which was just about the most awesomely insane thing I'd ever heard.

I saw Schneider at the North American Open pre-party but was too chicken to introduce myself. He was always surrounded by people and always looked like he was having a really good time—too good a time for a nobody like me to interrupt.

The competition started on Friday and had two categories: Difficulty and Speed. The emphasis, or the bulk of the prize money anyway, was on Difficulty. Competitors would be kept in Isolation until their turn, to prohibit them from gaining any beta on the route. The route itself was designed to be extremely difficult, with miniscule hand- and foot-holds requiring advanced sport-climbing technique along with extreme strength and endurance. One fall and you're out.

I waited in Isolation—a walled-off area outside, complete with a plywood bouldering wall for warm-up—with the others. When it was my turn, I took a moment to study the wall. It looked huge. Artificial walls somehow seem taller than their natural counterparts. The crux appeared to be a large overhang about two-thirds of the way up. The hand- and footholds looked sparse, forcing competitors to use technique—smooth, calculated movements and careful balance transfers—as opposed to just muscling their way up the wall.

I started strong, climbing carefully and deliberately. But after the first couple moves, I realized I wasn't going to make it to the top. The wall was just too tough for my current ability level. Still, I was a competitor at heart, so I kept climbing. I got about halfway up before peeling off the wall on a tiny crimper. The spirit was willing, as they say, but the flesh was weak.

Speed climbing was scheduled for the next day. The qualification round was certainly easier. We didn't even have to climb. Basically anyone who was already competing in Difficulty could sign up to compete in Speed. The race director took the first sixteen names, which luckily included mine.

On Saturday I showed up for the Speed competition not really sure what to expect. There was no Isolation area. We just hung out at the base of the wall. Another competitor named Nate Postma, who went on to found a successful artificial-climbing-wall company called Nicros, told me that we'd race each other up the wall, two at a time. Race? Now that was a concept I not only understood but thoroughly enjoyed. I figured Postma was pulling my leg. It sounded too good to be true.

A guy in a collared shirt walked over and explained the rules. We'd climb two at a time, on parallel routes. But we were really racing the clock, not each other. Once we got to the top, we'd lower back to the ground, swap routes, and do it again. The judges would rank competitors based on the summation of time for both routes climbed. The eight lowest scores would progress to the next round.

He told us to expect the routes to be more moderate than what we'd experienced in the Difficulty competition. They wouldn't be easy, but the point was to see who could make it to the top the fastest, not simply who could make it to the top. I was stoked. This was going to be fun.

When it was my turn, I don't think I even looked at my competitor. I was in the zone, similar to how I used to get at college track meets when it was my turn to pole-vault. I placed both hands and one foot on the wall, because that's what I'd seen everyone else do, and stared straight ahead. When the start gun went off, I flew up the wall. I don't think my belayer even had a chance to blink.

Both Postma and I made it to the next round. And the next. Then it was down to me and one other guy. But there wasn't much suspense—I won the North American Open Speed Climbing competition by a large margin. Having watched the others compete, I came up with a hypothesis on why I'd been so dominant. Climbers generally fit into one of two categories: old-school trad climbers or new-style sport climbers. And neither group, by design, was equipped for speed climbing.

The old-school guys climbed for the adventure of it, because they loved being outdoors, because living out of a van and climbing all day was their chosen form of rebellion. These were the guys who worshipped the glory days of Yosemite—the '60s and '70s, when Camp 4 was still a hippie haven. To them, climbing and competition were mutually exclusive concepts. They loved climbing particularly because it *wasn't* a competitive sport. They were at the North American Open more for curiosity than anything else. And while they didn't exactly love the Difficulty contest, they found it much more palatable than the Speed contest, which seemed obnoxious at best and the epitome of everything they hated about the world at worst. This group would eventually fall off the competition circuit altogether, after the novelty wore off.

Meanwhile, most of the new-school sport climbers were focused on difficulty, not speed. And while the two didn't seem to be mutually exclusive, I noticed that being good at the former did not automatically make you good at the latter. Difficulty climbers moved carefully, testing each hold, keeping three points of contact with the wall. Watching them do their thing, I came to understand that sport climbing is a very deliberate dance, and speed is not part of the routine. In fact, it is more the hallmark of a clumsy new climber. Difficulty climbers moved slowly and stealthily, like cats on the hunt. Climbing fast, for this group, was perhaps not only counterintuitive but also largely counterproductive.

The people who really liked speed climbing—with its fast pace and high drama—may have been the crowd. And me. My background seemed the perfect fit. I had an acquiescence to following the rules of the game (courtesy of playing varsity sports), a high degree of comfort on the wall (courtesy of the knee-quaking exposure on Yosemite's big walls), the skill to climb moderately difficult sport routes (courtesy of weekends spent at Joshua Tree and Mount Woodson), and a competitive spirit (courtesy of my genes, I guess). I couldn't wait for the next speed-climbing competition.

⚊⚊

As summer turned to fall in Los Angeles, I found myself increasingly less interested in my job. Or maybe it was that I was increasingly more interested in climbing at the expense of caring about my job. I did a weekend trip to Boulder, Colorado, to compete in the next nationals competition and again won Speed easily. I wished I could have stayed longer. The third indoor climbing wall in the nation had gone up in Boulder the year prior, and some of the best trad climbing in the United States can be had just outside of town in Eldorado Canyon State Park. I begrudgingly flew home to Los Angeles to go back to work.

At work my mind constantly wandered to climbing. Not the activity itself but rather calculating what it would take to climb full-time. I didn't have a mortgage or an expensive car. I'd already paid off my small college debt. My parents lived near San Francisco, so I could use their mailing address. And I had a good chunk of money saved from living below my means while working a yuppie job. At first it seemed like a pipe dream, but the more I went over it in my head, the more it started to make sense. Climbing, as a professional sport, was in its infancy, so why not try to get in at the beginning and see where it leads? I was 25 years old. I wasn't married. I didn't have any kids to support. The time was right.

I kept these thoughts to myself. I must have known, on some level, that friends and family would try to talk me out of it. Instead, I pulled my copy of *Atlas Shrugged*, a book I'd been exposed to in college, off the shelf and dove back in. The author, Ayn Rand, infuses her fiction with her life philosophy, known as objectivism. The heroes of her stories are achievers—men and women who use their talents to create art and ideas, build businesses, and invent technologies. I appreciated her idealistic message that the universe is open to human achievement and happiness, and that each person has within him the ability to live a rich, fulfilling, independent life. The book buoyed my confidence that it was okay to move forward with a plan that seemed ludicrous to everyone else but me. It was my life, and I needed to live it on my terms.

By the end of the year, I'd made up my mind. I was going to leave Parker Seals and take to the road, climbing six or seven days a week and competing in the 1990 national climbing series, which started in March in Berkeley. After a couple months I'd know if I'd made a good decision or needed to reevaluate.

Shortly after the New Year, my boss called me into his office. His boss was already inside. They sat me down to give me what they thought was good news. "Hans, we're really happy with your performance and hope this is the start of a long, lucrative career for you at Parker Seals. We'd like to offer you a promotion and a raise."

Shoot, I thought. Was I crazy to want to leave? I tried to smile as my bosses stared at me. I felt the weight of standing at a major crossroad. I knew the "right" decision was to man up, to leave behind the childish dream of becoming a professional rock climber, and to step into the successful business career that was mine for the taking. But still, I couldn't do it.

I took a deep breath, then told my boss no thank you. I explained, as best I could, that I was actually hoping to leave my job in order to do more rock climbing. He raised an eyebrow. "You know you're not going to make any money doing that," he said. We shared an awkward laugh.

That was my official two-week notice. Afterward, I outfitted my van with a futon mattress and drove to Tucson, where I'd heard the weather was mild enough to climb outside. There, I cragged alongside Bobbi Bensman. She was one of the strongest female climbers in the United States at the time, so I figured I was in a good spot to train. When I returned to California a couple weeks later, I was happy to discover that the state's first indoor climbing gym, City Rock, was opening in Berkeley, not too far from my parent's place. In March I competed in the Danskin Rockmaster and handily won Speed. I also did well in Difficulty, beating out my idol Steve Schneider and everyone else except Jim Karn, to take second. I wasn't bringing in much money, but I wasn't spending much money either. Climbing full-time was, so far, boding well for me.

Meanwhile, in Yosemite the spring climbing season was underway. The prevailing trend on big walls, catalyzed by Steve Schneider's ludicrous solo ascent of the Nose in less than 22 hours, seemed to be *climb 'til you drop*. Guys like Schneider, along with Dave Bengston, Scott Stowe, and Steve Gerberding, were more or less climbing themselves unconscious, and in doing so, setting new records on pretty much every route on El Capitan. Using the "single push" approach, they were whittling big-wall aid climbs that normally took six to eight days down to 30 hours or less.

To an outsider, this could be attributed to the sport-climbing influence—the Yosemite version of competitive climbing. But really, the two were unrelated. Ever since 1958 when Harding completed the Nose on El Capitan—the last remaining unclimbed big wall in Yosemite—climbers have been going back and repeating the original routes, trying to do them faster and more efficiently.

Case in point: In 1960 a team of four climbers—Royal Robbins, Chuck Pratt, Joe Fitschen, and Tom Frost—decided there was room for improvement over Harding's initial ascent of the Nose (forty-five days over a span of eighteen months, or for more of an apples-to-apples comparison, twelve days top to bottom on the final push). They also thought a different climbing technique would be more appropriate. Harding had used "siege tactics," a style popularized in the Himalayas—and still used on Everest today—that involves fixing lines between "camps." Hence, Harding had been able to return to the bottom to resupply food, water, and red wine (and to hack the legs off of stoves).

Robbins and team opted to climb the Nose "alpine" style, a continuous effort from bottom to top. It took them seven days (including six nights sleeping on the wall). The third ascent, in 1963 by Layton Kor, Steve Roper, and Glen Denny, took that time down to 3.5 days. Then, on May 26, 1975, the now-famous trio of Jim Bridwell, John Long, and Billy Westbay waged an all-out assault on the Nose, climbing it in the span of a single day, reportedly with enough time left over for dinner and drinks. The speed standard from that point forward became Nose in a Day, or "NIAD."

In 1985, two years after I started climbing, Duncan Critchley and Romain Vogler, both from Europe, set a new speed record on the Nose in an unbelievable 9 hours and 30 minutes. They'd averaged three pitches an hour. In comparison, it had taken me and Mike 46 hours to climb the Nose, which, after subtracting a few hours for sleeping, came out to roughly one pitch an hour.

As impressive as Critchley and Vogler's time was, at the rate Schneider and his cohorts were chewing up routes at the start of the Yosemite climbing season in 1990, the Nose record wouldn't hold much longer.

In April 1990 I drove to Seattle for the Danskin Rockmaster Finals. All the best sport climbers in the United States were there—Steve Schneider, Bobbi Bensman, Jim Karn, Dale Goodard. The only one missing was Ron Kauk—apparently, he'd graduated to the big leagues and was competing in Europe, along with America's best female climber, Lynn Hill.

I held my own in Difficulty, placing fifth, and won another landslide victory in Speed. I was feeling pretty good at the after-party, enough that when I saw Steve Schneider, I had the guts to say hello.

"Oh yeah, hey, you're the speed guy," he said and shook my hand.

We bantered a bit about Yosemite and the climbing comp scene, in that ironic, smart-alecky style common among like-minded men that usually indicates the start of a bromance. Things were going so well, in fact, that I blurted out that we should make a speedy ascent of the Nose together.

Steve responded with his signature giggle, an effervescent cackle that assures you he's laughing with you, not at you. "Yeah man, I'm in," he said. "If anything, just so you don't go do it without me."

In May I drove the van out to Yosemite to meet Steve. He lived in the employee housing at Camp 4, as part of the park's search and rescue team.

By coincidence, my parents were there car-camping, and it was Yosemite's one hundredth birthday. I'm pretty sure I failed to make a good first impression on Steve when the morning of the climb, my parents showed up at El Cap Meadow with a VHS recorder. They followed us through the woods to the base, with my dad in full narration mode: "How very fitting that Hans and Steve will be attempting to set a new speed record on Yosemite's number-one world-famous climb during the park's centennial," he said in his best news commentator voice.

At the foot of the Nose, my mom hugged me like I was leaving for the Army. My dad hovered around us with the VHS recorder, and photographer Ron Parks snapped close-ups with what appeared to be a very expensive, high-tech camera. I mumbled something by way of apology to Steve, but he didn't seem fazed. He pulled a small camera out of his backpack to show me. "It's cool. I brought mine too," he said.

"You guys feeling good?" my dad asked from behind the VHS recorder.

"We are feeling good, we are feeling *baaaad*, we are feeling fast," Steve said, hamming it up for the camera. I had a feeling he and I were going to get along just fine.

My contribution to our speed attempt was a big, fat digital watch that I wore around my ankle to keep it easily visible yet out of the way. Steve set the plan: The follower would carry the small backpack, which contained water and snacks. The leader would lead for several pitches in a row, to minimize lost time from changing out the lead. When we did change lead, it would be at a ledge or an otherwise easy place to stop. For the first lead, that spot would be Sickle Ledge, four pitches in.

I'm pretty sure Steve wanted to lead first. It just made good sense. The first four pitches, as I'd learned the hard way, are deceptively tricky, and he already had a handful of successful Nose climbs under his belt. But I was so out-of-my-mind excited that I don't think he had the heart to make me wait. So we started with me on lead at exactly 7 a.m.

I quickly figured out that speed climbing on the Nose was nothing like speed climbing on the competition wall at nationals. It's one thing to climb as hard as you can, gasping for air, on a 50-foot wall while protected by a toprope. Climbing that same way 300 feet above the ground while placing your own protection as you go is suicide. And while I certainly wanted to impress Steve Schneider, I didn't want to die trying.

On the first pitch, I focused more on efficiency than speed. Things were going well until the second pitch. I got to that same spot where Mike and I, on our first attempt, had a near catastrophic accident after swinging the wrong way on the pendulum. I didn't make the same mistake again; I knew to go right, not left. But after I swung over and began climbing up the new crack system, I neglected to place enough protection. Translation: I didn't want Steve to think I was a wuss, so I spaced my protection farther out than I normally would. And just like Murphy's Law predicts, I slipped and fell.

I was about 12 feet above the last piece of protection, which means I fell for double that distance, or 24 feet. Climbers call that long of a fall a "whipper," and it doesn't feel good, mentally or physically. But I was possessed by a different kind of terror: embarrassing myself in front of my idol, Steve Schneider.

I scrambled to straighten myself out—literally, I was hanging sideways in my harness. I thought that if I could resume climbing quickly, I would at least demonstrate that I could recover from a scare and keep my head in the game. Steve didn't mention the fall when we switched out the lead at Sickle Ledge, and I was only too happy to let it lie.

Steve cranked out his lead, and after four more pitches, we caught up to another team. I was shocked to discover it was Dave Bengston and Steve Gerberding—part of the "climb 'til you drop" club. They knew Steve, of course, but had no idea who I was. Speed climbing on artificial walls meant nothing in Yosemite. If Steve was the Jack Nicklaus of

Yosemite rock climbing, they must have assumed I was his caddy. Still, my confidence was bolstered by the fact that we were passing them. Even with my whipper, I was doing something right.

We reached the ledge under the Great Roof known as Camp IV, which Steve said was the approximate halfway point, at 11:26 a.m. I ran the numbers in my head—we were 4 hours and 26 minutes in, which put us on track to climb the entire route in a little under 9 hours. The record time was 9:30. Did I really have a shot at besting the speed record on the Nose on only my second ascent? The experienced college athlete in me said no way. I'd surely bonk on the second half of the climb. I was too far out of my league.

Steve didn't seem too worried about our time or my ability (or inability). But he did make one special request just before he led the Great Roof.

"Hans," he said. "I'm going to need you to stop calling me Steve and start calling me Shipoopi."

"Seriously?" I asked.

"Seriously," he said. "It's what my friends call me."

Then he started to sing the old song "Shipoopi" from *The Music Man*. And then he climbed the hellish crack leading up to the Great Roof like it was nothing. I heard him giggle at least twice.

At pitch 27 we switched the lead for the final time. Checking my watch, I was amazed that we were still in contention for the record. Steve looked me in the eye. "Bring 'er home, Hansie," he said.

"Anything for you, Shipoopi," I replied.

I felt like I had just enough gas left in the tank to go full throttle for the remaining 500 feet, and I went out of the gate fast and hard. Shipoopi tells a funny story of that moment—how my eyes narrowed and I became very still and then just tore up the route. I don't remember any of that. But

I do remember how I would reach up, not knowing where my hand would go, and somehow find a great hand jam, finger lock, or some other sturdy hold right at the apex of my reach, on nearly every single movement. Like magic. I would lift my foot up to a place where I knew there had been a good hold, without having to look down at my foot. I was learning how to "dance" up Yosemite granite. Looking back, I'm so grateful that Shipoopi was on my dance card that season in Yosemite. I went from rank amateur to knocking it around with Fred Astaire.

We topped out at 3:05 p.m., for a total time of 8 hours and 5 minutes. Sitting under the tree at the top, I did the math. My jaw dropped. "We beat them by an hour and 25 minutes!"

"Oh man, that's so cool," Shipoopi said. "Want to go get a sandwich?"

By sunset we were sitting in El Cap Meadow with my family enjoying sub sandwiches from Degnan's Deli and cold beer. My dad recorded post-climb interviews, and Ron shot more photos. Shipoopi said he felt like a star, and came up with the idea of us doing a climbing slideshow series named "The Blond Ambition Tour," pirating the name of pop star Madonna's most recent concert tour. From that point forward, I became "Hollywood Hans."

I didn't know it at the time, but once Bengston and Gerberding got off the wall, news of Shipoopi's and my speedy ascent of the Nose spread fast. A few days later another Yosemite climber named Peter Croft, along with climbing partner Dave Schultz, would usurp our record in a blistering time of 6:40.

A year later I returned to Yosemite to take it back. The race for the Nose was officially on.

CHAPTER 4

Learning the Croft

After the Venice Beach Climbing Competition the following year, in 1991, some of the best sport climbers in America were gathered beneath the freeway in Pasadena, California. We'd come to check out the "local crag"—60-foot columns supporting the highway. The area felt almost like a climbing gym, with graded routes up every column. "Care to make a small wager?" asked my friend Andres Puhvel, or Andy as he preferred to be called.

I couldn't hide my smile. Andy was the youngest of the group, a 19-year-old college student and a jovial but fierce competitor. The day before, he'd taken second to me in Speed, the fifth comp in a row. He was out for redemption.

"What do you have in mind?" I asked.

"One route, one chance, one winner," he said. Then, after a dramatic pause: "Loser hitchhikes naked on the highway."

I knew exactly who was responsible for the ridiculous stakes: Colorado climber Christian Griffith came around from behind a column with a huge grin on his face. "I've got just the route," he said. Christian was a route setter on the World Cup circuit and was well known in climbing circles for his penchant for the risqué. Case in point: He wanted to go for NIAD—Nose in a Day—clad only in one of his custom-designed G-strings.

Christian pulled out a quarter for the coin toss. "The hitchhiking has to last at least 10 seconds," he said, and flipped the coin.

"Heads!" Andy called. It was tails. He would have to climb first. I watched him stretch out his forearms, flipping his hands upside down and pulling his fingers back toward his wrist. He made a show of running in place, leering at me with an "eye of the tiger" stare. I managed to hold his gaze without cracking up. "You're going down, kid," I said.

Andy tied into the toprope and positioned himself on the wall in the official speed-climbing starting position—two hands and one foot on the route. George Squibb, another Colorado climber, was ready with the stopwatch: "Ready, set, go," he said.

Puhvel made quick work of the route, topping out in 47 seconds. "Not bad," I said as he lowered down. But I wasn't worried. I'd won every speed-climbing competition I'd entered since Snowbird in 1989, including the World Cup in Berkeley. Besides, I knew the routes under the highway in Pasadena pretty well, having trained there often.

When it was my turn, I flew up the route in 40 seconds. As my belayer lowered me to the ground, I stretched my arms into a victory V. Andy was waiting at the bottom with a high five and a grimace. "Looks like I'm dropping my drawers," he said. The group erupted into hoots and hollers. I watched in disbelief as Andy stepped out of his shorts, cupped both hands over his crotch, and scampered up to the highway. We all ran up after him, giggling like a bunch of schoolkids while he stood there with his thumb, and everything else, hanging out.

In that moment, I decided I had to climb the Nose with this guy. Andy had the drive, the skill, and the good humor that makes for the best kind of climbing partner. If he made it back down to the columns before dying of embarrassment, I was going to tell him so. Meanwhile, I joined the others in gleefully counting down from ten, nine, eight. . . .

Andy Puhvel came onto the climbing scene in 1986 at age 14. He climbed at Stoney Point, the crag nearest his parents' home in Los Angeles, during the school year and in Yosemite during the summers. He first scaled the Nose when he was 16, along with another 16-year-old named Ian Walker. The two teens did it in an impressive 36 hours. When he was 17 Andy went for NIAD with Kevin Thaw, and they got it handily in 11 hours. That was the year we met.

A climbing buddy, Reed Bartlett, and I had shown up at Stoney Point, a city park with large, sandstone boulders. The place was well known in climbing circles as the training ground for the Stonemasters, a hard-core group of 1970s Yosemite climbers that included John Bachar and John Long. In the late '80s and early '90s, it was one of the only climbing areas with sport-climbing routes in the 5.12 range. Reed and I were there to try the latest 5.12.

When we arrived at the route, a tall, gangly kid was already on it. Reed and I did an easier route while we waited and then took our turn on the 5.12. I worked my way up slowly, taking a couple falls as I figured out the moves. The teen stuck around to watch me work. When I came down, he introduced himself and told me his friend had made the first ascent of the route, naming it "Baby Clay" after the friend's newborn son. I realized I recognized Andy from local climbing competitions. We got to talking and before I knew it, we'd pulled out a watch, set up a toprope, and started trading off speed climbs.

Back and forth we went, mastering the moves, getting faster and faster. Andy whittled it down to 1 minute and 10 seconds—a time I couldn't beat. I wasn't too sore about it. Andy may not have been old enough to vote, but at 6 feet 7 inches tall and with three years of climbing in Yosemite under his belt, he had the body and mind of a more experienced climber. Plus, I genuinely liked him. Andy was contagiously enthusiastic about climbing and unapologetically competitive. He reminded me a little bit of myself.

I look back on our Stoney Point showdown as my first significant lesson on speed-climbing technique. At first, it took me about 15 minutes to ascend Baby Clay. But after repeated practice and some ego-stroking by young Mr. Puhvel, I pushed my time down to 1:30. There are huge gains to be had by practicing a route over and over, and, as I'd realize later, big walls like the Nose are no exception.

Andy was a freshman at the University of California–Santa Cruz when we made him hitchhike naked on Highway 210 in Pasadena. And after he'd completed the requisite 10 seconds, I asked him, in so many words, "Want to climb the Nose with me, so people don't *actually* think we're archrivals?" I didn't need to ask him twice.

Andy met me in Yosemite the day his college summer break started. Both of us knew there was a good chance we could climb the Nose faster than Shipoopi and I had the year prior. I think we both had our doubts that we could go faster than Peter Croft and Dave Schultz, but that didn't mean we weren't going to try. The time to beat was 6 hours and 40 minutes.

Andy was freaking out. "One rope?!" he said, for like the third time. We were in Yosemite just before sunrise, standing outside my van sorting our gear to climb the Nose. One rope meant we couldn't bail. The Nose's rappel anchors—the only way down—are spaced at 50 meters apart, too far to descend on one standard-size rope. With only one rope, we were 100 percent committed to getting to the top.

"For speed ascents, you only need one rope," I said. "Steve Schneider and I only brought one."

"But what if we need to go down?" Andy asked.

"Why would we need to go down?"

"I don't know, because someone is hurt, or, I don't know, sick. Like an emergency."

"Then I'll pay for your helicopter evacuation," I said. "If you're so wrecked that you can't follow me to the top on jugs, then you're probably too wrecked to rappel anyway."

Andy sighed. "You live in a van. You can't pay for that."

"Exactly why you should climb as safely as possible," I said.

"No second rope, no Andres Puhvel," Andy said.

"Fine," I muttered. "We'll bring a second rope."

Andy broke into a big grin. "Ha, I was just testing your loyalties. I'll be okay with just one rope. I think."

We started climbing as soon as the sun was up. I'd subdivided the route into six blocks. Andy led the first block, getting us up the first four pitches to Sickle Ledge. I took the next block to Dolt Tower at the top of pitch 11. Then we switched again and Andy took us through El Cap Tower, Texas Flake, Boot Flake, the King Swing, and the Grey Bands to Camp IV at the top of pitch 19.

While pitch 19 isn't the numeric halfway point of the thirty-one-pitch route, I'd learned from Shipoopi that it is roughly the halfway point in total time. According to my watch, Andy and I were crushing it. We were on track to best Shipoopi's and my time of 8:05. And while I didn't want to get my hopes too high, if things continued to go well, we would get really close to Croft and Schultz's time.

I took over the lead, moving us through the Great Roof and Pancake Flake to Camp V at pitch 24. We continued to move quickly and efficiently, taking sips of water from the bottles we had strung to our harnesses, and snacking steadily on the PowerBars we'd stuffed into the waistbands of our tights. I didn't want to pressure Andy when we switched out the lead, but we were making exceptional time. "Dude, we might beat Croft and Schultz," I said.

Andy's eyes widened. "Holy shit, holy shit, holy shit," he muttered as he prepared to lead his final block.

Andy led us up the next couple pitches, including the dicey one immediately off Camp V that spooked me on my first ascent with Mike, and on to Camp VI at the top of pitch 26. Andy didn't lose momentum but had flamed himself with the effort. "I can barely open my hands," he told me, struggling to switch out the lead with his gnarled fists. Luckily, it was my turn. We were 500 feet from the top, and I felt a burst of energy.

I moved as quickly and safely as possible through the next four pitches. Every muscle in my body was on fire. By the time I reached the start of the final pitch—the bolt ladder on the overhanging wall to the top—I understood what Andy meant about not being able to open his hands. Mine were suddenly useless. I checked the time.

Holy hell. Not only were we going to beat Croft and Schultz, but depending on how fast I moved, we might beat them by as much as a half hour. The problem was my hands. They weren't exactly working. Andy was jugging his way up to meet me, but I didn't want to lose time switching out the lead. Besides, based on how Andy's hands felt after leading his last block, he wasn't going to be in any condition to take over.

I was desperately shaking my hands out when the idea hit me. I grabbed a sling off my harness and wrapped one end around my wrist. I attached a carabiner to the other end. Then I twisted the sling until it cinched down. I worked my way up the bolt ladder using the carabiner like a claw—clipping it into an overhead bolt and hanging off my wrist while I moved my feet up to the next bolt. Every few bolts, I paused to clip in a quickdraw, followed by my rope for protection. The method worked beautifully, despite frying my biceps and shoulders. But I made it to the lip, scrambling over it and clipping into the anchor. My heart was hammering when I called down "off belay" to Andy. Now it was all up to him.

I sat at the finishing anchor, eyes glued to the watch. When Andy crested the lip, he had a huge smile on his face. I was already jumping up and down. Our time was 6:03. We had beaten two of the greatest Yosemite climbers of all time by 37 minutes.

During the hike down from the top, I fantasized about the article that *Climbing* magazine might want to write about us. Two nobodies from LA had usurped the legendary team of Croft and Schultz. I called my mom and told her to be ready to buy the local newspaper. Later that afternoon in El Cap Meadow, I worked on my tan and combed lemon juice through my hair. Andy made fun of me. I didn't care. Hollywood Hans was having his moment.

But there was no newspaper article for my mom to buy because Croft and Schultz reclaimed the record within a week—in an incredible 4:48. To add an exclamation point, they did it as part of a larger project: the first one-day "linkup" of the Nose and the Salathé Wall. A linkup is a back-to-back climb: Croft and Schultz climbed the Nose, hiked down, and then immediately climbed the Salathé, all in less than 24 hours.

The Salathé is the next route over from the Nose. Royal Robbins, Tom Frost, and Chuck Pratt established it as the second significant "big-wall" route up El Capitan when they climbed it in 1961. Like the Nose, the Salathé is considered a classic, and like the Nose, it takes experienced climbers about four days to ascend. Some argue that it's even better than the Nose, as it follows the most natural line up El Cap. I contend that the Nose is more classic, as it goes dead center up the prow of the cliff, but I may be biased.

At that time I considered Croft and Schultz's new record on the Nose untouchable. No one would ever be able to beat it, except, perhaps, they themselves. It was an hour and 15 minutes faster than Andy and I had done it, and I was pretty sure we couldn't have climbed the Nose any faster than we did. Just to be sure, we tried again a couple days later. Not only did we not come anywhere near Croft and Schultz's record, but we climbed it 14 minutes *slower* than our previous time of 6:03.

I decided to give it a rest . . . sort of. I'd been dating climber Nancy Feagin for a couple months, and she was game to set a male-female speed record on the Nose. At the time, there were no documented times; there wasn't even an Internet. I asked around and found out that the year prior, in 1990, Merry Braun had become the first woman to climb NIAD, along with her husband Werner Braun, who was both one of the original Stonemasters and a member of Yosemite's search and rescue team. I tracked down Werner somewhere between the cafeteria and the designated SAR plots at the end of Camp 4, where he lived, to find out the details of his and Merry's ascent.

"Our exact time?" said Braun, looking confused as he ran his hand through his constantly tousled hair. "It's not like I had a watch. We started at sunrise, and we topped out shortly after dark."

Nancy and I climbed the Nose together in August, in 10 hours and 5 minutes, setting the first "officially timed" male-female speed record. She hadn't done the Nose in a single push before but was a strong, experienced, fearless climber. The route was starting to feel familiar to me; or at least some of the techniques that I'd struggled with on earlier ascents were becoming less awkward. When we topped out, I realized how much fun I'd had witnessing another climber tackling NIAD for the first time. I'd thoroughly enjoyed helping Nancy get acquainted with all the quirks and thrills of the route. I didn't know it at the time, but I was falling in love. With the Nose.

I'd gotten a taste of the World Cup scene in Europe the year before, competing in Germany, France, and Spain. The level of skill, the size of the crowd, the amount of prize money, and the number of sponsorships were leagues beyond what we had in the United States. But I hadn't done very well in the Difficulty category, and none of the events I had competed in had included Speed.

For the 1991 season, I'd heard there would be a speed competition at the World Cup in Clusone, Italy, on August 30, as well as at the first-ever Climbing World Championship in Frankfurt. Thanks to my dirtbag lifestyle, my savings from my yuppie job were still holding, so after Nancy and I climbed the Nose, I bought a plane ticket and flew to Italy.

I was interested to see if I could hold my own in speed in Europe. When I won in Clusone, the general consensus seemed to be that I'd won "only because Jacky Godoffe wasn't there." The famous French climber had never lost a speed-climbing competition. We would meet for the first time at the World Championship in Frankfurt.

All of the best climbers in the world showed up in Frankfurt. François Legrand and Isabelle Patissier from France, Yuji Hirayama from Japan, Lynn Hill from the United States. It was impossible not to feel nervous. Like all the other speed-climbing competitions I'd ever done, there were sixteen of us to start. In Isolation I saw the highly regarded Jacky Godoffe up close for the first time. He was hard to miss—super-skinny with bright orange hair.

"The American champion, we meet at last," he said with a thick French accent when I introduced myself. There was not a hint of insincerity in his voice. As we made small talk, I realized that he was not only friendly but warm and funny. I felt more at ease.

Round 1 was the "seeding" round. We were brought out in pairs to climb side by side on two parallel routes, and, similar to Snowbird, immediately switched routes and did it again. Each climber's score would be a summation of his total time on both routes. I was thrilled at the "race" format, and didn't bother to hide my happiness—having another person next to me makes me climb faster.

I placed second in the seeding round, which determined my "bracket" for the remainder of the competition. If I made it all the way through, I would race Jacky, who'd been seeded first, in the finals. Back in Isolation, we all agreed that the route on the left was slightly harder than the route on the right. And I realized that unlike in the American competitions that I'd won by a comfortable margin, the competition was fierce. Salavat Rakhmetov was among the climbers in my bracket, a burly Russian who had lost Speed only once in his professional career—to Jacky.

When I came out for the next round, the crowd was starting to get rowdy. I loved their energy, and I climbed really well, progressing all the way to the finals. I got to watch Salavat beat out his competitor to take third, and then it was time for me and Jacky to face off.

Spontaneously, the Frenchman and I decided to play up the drama. Instead of starting with both hands and one foot on the wall, we backed up a few feet and took a running start. The crowd went wild. Jacky hit his buzzer a moment before I did, but I was on the harder left-side route, so it was still anyone's match.

When we switched routes, the noise from the crowd drowned out any thoughts in my head. I climbed the second route on pure instinct, hitting the buzzer just before Jacky. When we lowered down, neither of us knew who had won. At the awards ceremony shortly after, we found out it was me, by a fraction of a second. And so I became the first-ever Speed Climbing World Champion. I still have the trophy. But the $500 in German deutsche marks are long gone.

I stayed in Europe to finish out the rest of the World Cup series. During those couple months, I noticed how closely sport climbers in

Europe followed the Yosemite scene. In the United States sport climbing and trad climbing had become pretty divided. But in Europe it seemed all the sport climbers knew who Peter Croft was and that he had the speed record on the Nose, among other accomplishments. They loved hearing my story of how Steve Schneider and I set a new Nose record, only to lose it a few days later to Croft, and then how Andy and I took it back, only to lose it again to Croft in less than a week. Countless European climbers told me it was one of their greatest dreams to climb the Nose.

In retrospect, those conversations marked the first time I understood how highly regarded Yosemite was by the international climbing community—that it is, without a doubt, the greatest climbing area on earth. I remember feeling gratitude that I grew up with it practically in my backyard. My appreciation for Yosemite, for El Capitan, and for the Nose was deepening.

Those feelings intensified when I accompanied my climbing friend Doug Englekirk to Lynn Hill's new house in Provence, France. Before Lynn had become one of the best sport climbers in the world, she cut her teeth climbing in Yosemite in the 1970s, including sending the Nose in 1979. We started swapping Yosemite stories and had a hard time stopping. Being the small world that climbing is, one of Lynn's old boyfriends was John Long, part of the famous trio, along with Billy Westbay and Jim Bridwell, who had made the first one-day ascent of the Nose in 1975, coining the term NIAD.

At the end of December, I got bad news from home. I'd called my parents to wish them a merry Christmas. Those were the days before mobile phones and e-mail, so my contact with them while I was in Europe had been limited. I learned that my dad had been diagnosed with cancer. What he'd assumed was the ordinary back pain that comes with aging turned out to be a large tumor. I flew home right away and got to spend a few weeks with my dad before he died at age 58.

After his initial surprise at me leaving my job to become a rock climber, my dad had been steadily building a reputation as my biggest fan. He was there when I got the Nose speed record for the first time with Shipoopi, not only narrating from behind the VHS recorder but manning the tripod for 8 hours straight in El Cap Meadow. He attended every climbing competition in San Francisco's Bay Area, usually with the video camera in tow. The local climbing community is tight-knit, and by February it seemed everyone knew my dad had died. Friends assumed I wouldn't travel to Vancouver for the upcoming climbing comp because I was "mourning."

I thought about it some. It wasn't lost on me that it was almost exactly a year since I'd left Parker Seals. If anything, my dad's death reinforced the fact that I'd done the right thing. Life is too short to put off doing the things you love. "Later" is never guaranteed. So I went to Vancouver and then to the Phoenix Bouldering Competition after that. I got the impression that some people believed I was "distracting" myself from the pain of losing my father. But I felt like being engrossed with climbing—the travel, the training, the planning of new projects—was a way to let my father's passing have a positive effect on my fledgling climbing career. By late spring I was back in Yosemite, where the Nose, like an old friend with a funny story to tell about my dad and his VHS recorder, awaited.

In Yosemite my interest in speedy ascents of the Nose was reignited when Andy introduced me to one of his climbing partners—the guy he'd done NIAD with, Kevin Thaw. Climbers in Yosemite Valley were a fairly small tribe, and I'd already heard good things about Kevin from another one of his climbing partners, Shipoopi, who was rapidly becoming my best friend.

Kevin and I set out on a temperate morning in May, using the same technique that Andy and I had: leading in blocks with just one rope, having the follower carry one small backpack for the extra water and snacks, climbing as hard as we could, and transitioning between leads as efficiently as we could. Kevin was an incredibly competent climber, strong and fast. I couldn't have asked for a better partner. But in the end we climbed the Nose in 6 hours and 1 minute—just 2 minutes faster than Andy and I had done it.

Croft and Schultz's record time of 4:48 continued to boggle my mind. At night, while relaxing in my van shortly before falling asleep, I'd break the Nose out pitch by pitch in my head. I'd dissect it like a manufacturing process at Parker Seals, hunting for places where I could remove inefficiencies. I'd always end up at the same conclusion: There weren't any.

Maybe it was a matter of fitness. Croft and Schultz had done the climb an hour and 15 minutes faster than Andy and me, or roughly 2.5 minutes faster per pitch. They were more experienced on big walls, and it logically followed that they were stronger, faster, and had better endurance on long routes. Perhaps I just needed more practice.

I kept hoping I'd run into Croft or Schultz in the valley and somehow find the courage to ask their opinions. But I never saw them—not in the El Cap Meadow, not in the Camp 4 parking lot, not at Degnan's Deli. Eventually, I found out why: Schultz wasn't in the valley, he was elsewhere working on a film. And Croft hadn't been in the valley much either. He was in the midst of doing a series of slideshows about his climbing experiences. I poked around a bit more and found that his next appearance was in Santa Barbara, 6 hours away. I decided to make the drive to hear him speak. Maybe I could glean a tidbit or two about his technique on the Nose. I like to think of it as a fact-finding mission. Shipoopi decreed me "Hollywood Hans the Stalker."

Sitting through Peter Croft's slideshow on May 15, 1992, in Santa Barbara, I came to a new level of respect for him. I learned that in 1985, he did the first "free solo"—the term for climbing up a rock wall without any gear or even a rope for protection—on the Rostrum, a 5.11c-crack climb in Yosemite that spans eight pitches over the course of 800 vertical feet. Two years later he did the first free solo of Astroman, another 5.11c in Yosemite, this time eleven pitches and 1,100 feet. People sometimes confuse "free soloing" with "free climbing." The former, what Peter was doing, is crazy hard-core. The latter means "free from aid," so you can't insert any gear to grab or stand on, but you still use a rope for protection.

Peter was also responsible, along with John Bachar, for the first one-day linkup of the Nose and Half Dome, and then, with Dave Schultz in 1991, the first one-day linkup of the Nose and Salathé Wall (the same climb where they took the Nose speed record down to 4:48). Also in 1991 Peter did the first free ascent of Moonlight Buttress, a 5.12d sandstone crack climb encompassing nine pitches and 1,000 feet in Zion National Park. The American Alpine Club awarded him the Robert and Miriam Underhill Award—the most prestigious award for mountaineering in the United States.

Peter Croft was at a level of climbing beyond anyone I had ever encountered. Forget the speed record on the Nose, I was clearly out of my league. The best I could hope for was to climb with him someday. After the show I stuck around to say hello and shake his hand. When I introduced myself, Peter actually knew who I was—a fact that put a perma-grin on my face the rest of the week. He was so cool and so friendly that I blurted it out before I could stop myself: "Hey, we should climb together sometime."

He didn't flinch: "Sure thing."

Afterward, I stressed about how to make official plans with Peter. I wanted to climb with him right away, but I didn't want to embarrass myself by being overeager. At the same time, I didn't want to wait too long—what if he forgot he'd mentioned it and I lost my chance? Or what if he was "just being nice" and didn't really want to climb with me? Peter didn't have a phone, so I'd have to hunt him down in person. That could be really awkward if he'd just been being nice. I decided that the next time I saw him, I would wait to see if he mentioned climbing together, then I'd know he really meant it.

"What is this, high school?" laughed Shipoopi, upon hearing my plan.

He was right. I wrote "talk to Peter Croft" in my planner, like that would help make it happen. Then, on June 4, I went and climbed the Salathé with my girlfriend Nancy. We did it fast, in 12:15, setting a male-female speed record. It was the perfect stress release.

The valley was crowded, so Nancy and I drove 30 miles to Tuolumne at the north end of the park and stayed at White Wolf Campground. As luck would have it, I ran into Peter the very next day. Despite all my doubts, I felt confident enough to mention climbing together. Peter was game, and we made plans for the Nose on June 7. The day before, I felt kind of giddy. I was going climbing with Peter Croft.

Peter met me at El Cap Meadow at twilight. He wore a T-shirt and shorts and carried a single bottle of water. As we walked over to the base, he explained that we'd lead in blocks and his plan for climbing the first block to Sickle Ledge.

"I'll lead and we'll short fix," he said.

I had an idea what he was talking about, but wasn't totally sure.

"Okay," I said, trying to play it cool. Then, realizing my life was at stake, I added, "Just tell me what I need to do."

If Peter balked at my ignorance, he didn't let on. "When I get to the top of the first pitch, I'll set up an anchor and fix the line for you to jug up, just like the follower normally does. But instead of standing around waiting for you to finish, I'll start climbing the second pitch."

I was quiet for a moment while I thought it through. If I was busy jugging up the first pitch, who was belaying Peter? "I'll be self-belaying," he said, as if reading my mind. "With this." He jangled the Grigri hanging from his harness.

Petzl had debuted the Grigri, a revolutionary new belay device, the year prior. Unlike the stitch plates we'd all been using up until that point, a Grigri has a built-in braking function. It works by way of an internal cam, which, if the rope is yanked too quickly (as in a fall), rotates and pinches the rope so it can't move any farther. Otherwise, the cam allows the rope to feed through steadily as the lead climber ascends. While Peter's method of using a Grigri to self-belay wasn't what Petzl intended, I was engineering-minded enough to know it would work.

"So what happens when I get to the top of the first pitch?" I asked.

"Pretty much the same as usual—you'll clip into the anchor, and put me on belay," he said. "The difference is that I'll be over your head, already climbing. So just make sure you put the rope leading up to me on belay. Then untie the rest of the rope from where I fixed it at the anchor."

Brilliant. This was one of his tricks to speed climbing the Nose. I was going to learn a ton.

Using Peter's fixed-rope method, we made it to Sickle Ledge in 25 minutes. Four pitches in 25 minutes, and that included passing Nancy and Sue McDevitt, who were in the process of doing the first NIAD by women (they'd finish later that day in 17:40). I was speechless. At the rate we were going, we'd be done before lunchtime.

Peter peeled off his shirt and tossed it down. Then we switched out the lead. "We should be able to simul-climb for a couple," he said.

Uh-oh. I'd tried simul-climbing—a technique borrowed from mountaineering where both climbers are roped together and move simultaneously up the same pitch—once, in 1990, with Andy. It was faster but considerably more dangerous. We were climbing the third pitch on the Salathé Wall, and I was leading. About halfway up the pitch, Andy fell due to pulling a piece I had placed. In simul-climbing if the follower falls, he sucks the leader off the wall too. One moment I was steadily climbing a 5.9 slab, and the next I was plummeting 10 feet down to the last piece of protection I'd placed. My fall was not only completely unexpected, and thus terrifying, but also rather violent. The granite rock face bruised my arms and legs, and the rope slashed a good-size welt into my thigh. After that I'd decided simul-climbing was too sketchy and should be reserved for rare occasions.

But now Peter Croft was recommending it as part of our strategy for climbing the Nose. I couldn't say no. I reminded myself that Peter was the follower on this next block, and barring some freakish accident, he wasn't going to fall. I should be safe. In theory, anyway. I gathered up my courage and took over the lead.

I managed to block out my initial apprehension by concentrating hard on my lead, free-climbing the easy stuff, aid-climbing the hard stuff, and "French-freeing"—the sardonic term derived from the traditional way to climb in the Alps—whenever I could by stepping on fixed gear and grabbing stuck cams left behind in the cracks. I soon started to relax. This wasn't so bad. Peter stayed within easy earshot, and I felt really safe with him. By the end of the next four pitches, I was getting into the groove and even enjoying myself.

We switched out the lead for pitch 8, where the Stove Legs crack system begins. I was now on "the back end" of the rope and thus clipped the Grigri to my belay loop and then threaded the rope through it. Once Peter had placed three pieces of gear, which put him at about 40 feet overhead, I began following. When he reached the crack, I noticed he sped up. No big surprise there—Peter was known as a master crack climber. I kicked it into another gear, navigating the crack as fast as I could, stopping only to pluck out the pieces of protection Peter had placed as I went by them. I was working hard but with a smile. I felt like I was holding my own. And I was loving it.

At least until the second pitch of Stove Legs, when I noticed that Peter had "run out" his protection. There had to be at least 20 feet—way too much space—in between the piece of pro I was retrieving from the crack and the next one Peter had placed above it. I suddenly didn't feel so safe anymore. I tried to calm myself down. Well, hell, I thought, this is Peter Croft. He climbs thousand-foot-high cracks rated 5.11 and 5.12 without any protection at all. The 5.9/5.10-rated Stove Legs must have been a walk in the park for him.

But it wasn't a walk in the park for me. What happened if I fell? He could get seriously injured if I ripped him that far down the wall. Maybe Peter had overestimated my skills. My inner monologue continued; worrying as I climbed. The last straw was the next time I looked up and saw just one piece of protection between the two of us. Good lord. Just one piece of protection that, in the case of a fall, would be called upon to save the lives of two men.

"Hey Peter," I called up, "maybe a few more pieces of pro?"

"You got it," he said and immediately put in another piece.

I exhaled.

Peter kept to his word on the rest of the Stove Legs, placing more conservative protection. It slowed us down a bit but only minimally. We reached Dolt Tower in 1 hour and 25 minutes. The first time I successfully climbed the Nose, three years ago with Mike, it took us more than 12 hours to get to the very same spot.

Peter and I moved through the rest of the route using a combination of short-fixing and simul-climbing, and even some plain old ordinary climbing. Some features, like the King Swing, Great Roof, and "Changing

Corners" in the upper dihedral, were not practical to do any other way. Peter lead the last pitch—the bolt ladder to the lip—in the traditional manner, anchoring in at the top and fixing the line for me to jug it. After he called down "off belay," I was shaking as I switched out my gear from belaying to jugging. Now it was all up to me.

"Line fixed," Peter said. That was my cue that it was safe to begin. His voice was like a starting gun going off in a speed-climbing comp. I went fully anaerobic as I jugged the line up the overhang, gasping for air and grunting out loud as my arms struggled to support my entire body. I heaved myself over the lip. Total time: 4:22. We'd broken Peter's previous record by 26 minutes. I whooped, I hollered, I charged Peter and engulfed him in a huge bear-hug, never mind that he was topless, soaked in sweat, and not a hugger. I'd just had the greatest climb of my life.

As we hiked down, Peter mused over what climbing he was going to do in the afternoon.

"Seriously?" I said.

"Well, it's not even 11 a.m.," he said.

As we talked more, I started to understand Peter's motivation. He climbed quickly because it enabled him to climb *more* in a given day. It wasn't so much about speed records; in fact, Peter admitted that he and Dave had been pretty clueless about the Nose speed record. When they bested Shipoopi's and my time in 1990, they'd been climbing it fast to try and link up the Nose and the Salathé in less than 24 hours, which they ultimately failed to accomplish on that attempt. It was the same story when they took the record back from me and Andy in 1991, only that time they succeeded in the linkup. I realized that we'd never been competitors, more like colleagues, and that collaboration made for some truly great climbing. Our speed record on the Nose would stand for nine years.

CHAPTER 5

Going Solo

Shortly after Peter Croft and I set a new speed record on the Nose, Lynn Hill showed up in Yosemite. "The word on the street is that she's looking to free the Nose," Shipoopi told me.

Free climbing means "free from aid." Free climbers don't use aiders or other gear to ascend, only the natural features of the rock, jamming their fists into cracks, crimping edges, slotting their fingers into small divots, and standing on micro-edges the width of a quarter. Not to be confused with free soloing, free climbers still use a rope for protection and carry pro—nuts, hexes, and cams—to insert into the rock to secure the rope as they climb.

Climbers have been experimenting with free climbing in Yosemite since the 1960s. On big-wall routes like the Nose, it was more of a piece-meal effort. The Nose's obvious cracks, like the Stove Legs, had already been freed by the Stonemasters. But other features on the route, like the Great Roof, were presumed impossible to do without aid, even by the best climbers of the day. For the Nose to "go free," someone would need to figure out how to free-climb every section and then string it all together in one climb.

If anyone could do it, Lynn Hill could. She started competing in Europe in 1986 and went on to win more than thirty international comps.

In 1991 she free-climbed Masse Critique in France and in doing so became the first woman to climb a 5.14 anywhere in the world.

I ran into Lynn myself a couple days later near the cafeteria and extended an invitation to do a one-day speed ascent of the Nose. She was down. We met up on a bluebird morning in July. As we hiked to the base of El Capitan, Lynn confirmed that she was considering free-climbing the Nose. "Do you think it's possible?" she asked.

"Maybe," I said. "But not today."

Lynn laughed. "Okay, Hans, not today. But I want to do some reconnaissance for it, so I'm not making any promises on speed either."

"You got it, Lynn."

I wasn't worried about her speed. Lynn is one of the best climbers in the world, so we'd be climbing Nose in a Day at the very least. I had geared up for a standard NIAD ascent, with one rope and one backpack to hold the food and extra water. I suspected that we would improve on Nancy's and my time of 10:05 to set a new male-female speed record.

Lynn and I swung leads, trading off at the top of each pitch. When we got to pitch 13, just beneath El Cap Tower, I pointed out Jardine's Traverse, a detour that was originally intended to enable free climbing. Ray Jardine, the same visionary who created the spring-loaded camming devices called Friends that made climbing the Nose safer and easier, also aspired to free-climb it. He went to work trying to figure out how to make that possible in 1981.

One of free climbing's biggest barriers on the Nose was the King Swing—the audacious 100-foot pendulum. The sequence begins at El Cap Tower, climbing up Texas Flake, navigating the bolt ladder across the blank granite face in between Texas and Boot Flake, climbing up the back of Boot Flake, then lowering down the front side and taking a giant swing to the left to reach the next crack system. Ray's idea was to forget all that and instead traverse over to the next crack system straight from El Cap Tower. Free climbers could then work their way up the crack, eventually reaching the same spot they'd end up at after the King Swing but with considerably less monkeying around.

The only problem was that in between El Cap Tower and the next crack system was a 35-foot swatch of sheer, smooth granite—not unlike the one in between Texas Flake and Boot Flake that requires a bolt ladder for aid climbers to cross. Since Ray was trying to create a way to free-climb the Nose, adding a bolt ladder in between El Cap Tower and the crack didn't make sense. Instead he went up with a hammer and chisel and chipped away a few hand- and footholds to bridge the blank face.

Many people in the climbing community (including Lynn) felt that Ray's man-made traverse was in poor form, that imposing one's will upon the rock by making physical alterations wasn't in keeping with the spirit of free climbing. Ray got so much backlash for "picking the Nose" that he ended up abandoning the project. It would be another decade before someone seriously attempted to free-climb the Nose again.

Lynn paused to contemplate Jardine's Traverse, which would be her route when she attempted to free-climb the Nose. "You going to avoid all Ray's handiwork?" I asked.

Lynn wrinkled her nose. "I'll climb it as-is," she said. "I can't erase history."

We continued through the traditional sequence, enjoying the adventure of ascending flakes and swinging across a granite cliff while suspended 1,500 feet above the ground. I realized then that while I supported others' attempts to free the Nose, I wasn't interested in sacrificing even one of its fun, quirky features to do so. I liked the Nose pretty much exactly as it was.

When we reached the top of pitch 22, just before the Great Roof, Lynn stopped. To date, no one had been able to figure out how to free-climb the

Great Roof. It starts as a small crack, shooting straight up the center of a corner for 100 feet. Then the crack tilts right, snaking beneath a behemoth overhang (the "roof") for about 30 feet. There were places in the upper reaches of the pitch where the crack narrowed so much that it was unlikely to fit even a pinky finger.

I watched Lynn study the crack. "This is where Brooke got hung up," she said. She was referring to Brooke Sandahl, a talented free climber who, in 1991, made the first serious bid to free-climb the Nose in its entirety since Ray Jardine. Brooke, along with Scott Franklin, had made it across Jardine's Traverse and got all the way to the Great Roof before reverting back to aid climbing. He came back the following year and tried again with Dave Schultz but to the same end.

I led the pitch the regular aid-climbing way and then anchored in so Lynn could jug up. She wasn't moving markedly slower than usual, but something about her demeanor had changed. She'd gone from light-hearted to laser-focused. I could practically see her mind spinning as she ascended, processing the features of the rock, imagining how she would free-climb it.

When the crack turned and dove beneath the roof, Lynn stopped and traced the sliver with her finger. Then she glanced down, presumably scanning for footholds. She did the same about two-thirds of the way beneath the roof. When she reached the anchor, her eyes were wide. "Wow, there's literally nothing there," she said. The rock face beneath the roof appeared devoid of footholds, and the crack itself was even smaller than she'd remembered from her first Nose ascent in 1979.

"Could you even get your fingers in there?" I asked.

"Barely," she said, "but I've got a secret weapon." She held up one tiny hand. At 5 feet 1.5 inches tall and not even 100 pounds, Lynn had perhaps the only fingers on earth both small enough and strong enough to free-climb the Great Roof.

My first go at the Nose record, with Steve Schneider, aka Shipoopi, in 1990.
RON PARKS

The image of me and Peter Croft (and my van) that appeared the size of a post-age stamp in *Climbing* magazine in 1992, along with the news that we'd broken the Nose record.

Getting ready to climb the Nose with Lynn Hill in 1992, as reconnaissance for her future free-climbing attempt. We set a new male-female speed record that day, in 8:40. RON PARKS

The 20 in 20 Team: Nancy Feagin, Willie Benegas, Christian Santelices, and me. We climbed 20 classic routes in 20 days in the summer of 1993.

Mark Melvin and me at the top of the Nose after our first run up it together in 1995. He would climb it four more times with me.

Hundreds of climbers gathered in Yosemite in 2000 to celebrate Camp 4 being put on the list of historic registered sites. Some of them pictured here: Jose Pereyra, Ron Kauk, Peter Mayfield, Mike Corbett, Randy Leavitt, Scott Burke, Ed Barry, Syble Hechtel, Peter Croft, Todd Skinner, John Bachar, Rick Sylvester, Rick Cashner, and Ken Yager.

Exhausted and elated after rope-soling the linkup—the Regular Northwest Face on Half Dome and the Nose of El Capitan—in 1999, in less than 24 hours.

Jacki and I were married in El Cap Meadow on October 7, 2000. MIKE AYON

Playing with my firstborn, Marianna, in El Cap Meadow.

Posing with Erik Weihenmayer, his guide dog Seigo, Sam Bridgem, and Jeff Evans, the team for the first (and only) blind ascent of the Nose.
ELLEN WEIHENMAYER

Getting manhandled by the Wall Rats, Scott Cory, Beth Rodden, and Tori Allen, at the top of El Capitan in 2001.
ROB RAKER

Rossano Boscarino, Thomas Huber, and I adoring the Nose from El Cap Meadow.

My wife, Jacki, in 2002, working her way up the chimney behind Texas Flake on the first female roped-solo ascent of the Nose.

TECH SCHOOL: TAME ICE WITH NEW-WAVE TIPS

ROCK & ICE
THE CLIMBER'S MAGAZINE
NO.121
JANUARY 15, 2003

Possessed
Hans Florine's rage
against time

Great Unknowns
The best crags you've
never heard of

Mayhem in Nepal
Maoist rebels nab climbers

SuperTopo
Zion's BIG 5 routes

Hans Florine speed
climbing El Cap's Nose

New
AAC's Accidents in America
learn from others' mistakes

The *Rock & Ice* cover from January 2003, after Yuji Hirayama and I set a new speed record on the Nose, breaking the three-hour barrier in 2:48:55.
ROCK & ICE

The Nose
VI 5.10 C2

31
30 5.10c/C1
29 5.10d/C1
28 5.10c/C1
27 The
    Changing
    Corners
    5.13c/C1
Camp VI 26
    5.11b/C2
25 The Glowering Spot
    5.12r/C2
Camp V 24
    5.11c/C2
23 Pancake
    Flake
5.11c/C1
22
The Great Roof
    5.9 d/C1
21 5.9
Camp IV 20
    5.11c/C2 19 5.10d/C2
18
    17 16 Boot Flake
5.10c/C1   5.10c/C1
Eagle Ledge 17
The King Swing   15 Texas Flake
                     5.9
                 14 El Cap Tower
                 5.7
Jardine Traverse 13
                  5.9
                12 5.8
Dolt Tower 11
            5.10c
            10
            5.10b
        9
    The Stove Legs
    5.10b
        8
        5.8
Dolt Hole 7
          7 5.9
        6
        5.9/C1
        5
        4Cl
        4 Sickle Ledge
    5.11c/C2
        3
    5.10c/C2
        2
    5.10d/C1
        1
    5.11/C1

© MARK HUDON 2012, ELCAPPANOS.COM

After the Hubers captured the speed record in 2007, I took them for beers. I used the $100 I won in a wager with Bob Yoho, in which I bet that someone would break Yuji's and my record.

In 2008, Yuji and I made the front page of the *San Francisco Chronicle*, stealing Obama's thunder during the Democratic primary. PAUL HARA

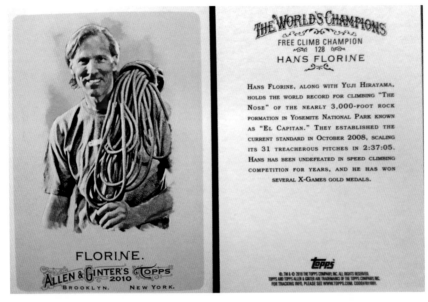

THE WORLD'S CHAMPIONS
FREE CLIMB CHAMPION
128
HANS FLORINE

HANS FLORINE, ALONG WITH YUJI HIRAYAMA,
HOLDS THE WORLD RECORD FOR CLIMBING "THE
NOSE" OF THE NEARLY 3,000-FOOT ROCK
FORMATION IN YOSEMITE NATIONAL PARK KNOWN
AS "EL CAPITAN." THEY ESTABLISHED THE
CURRENT STANDARD IN OCTOBER 2008, SCALING
ITS 31 TREACHEROUS PITCHES IN 2:37:05.
HANS HAS BEEN UNDEFEATED IN SPEED CLIMBING
COMPETITION FOR YEARS, AND HE HAS WON
SEVERAL X-GAMES GOLD MEDALS.

FLORINE.
ALLEN & GINTER'S TOPPS
BROOKLYN.   NEW YORK.
2010

After Yuji Hirayama and I set the speed record on the Nose in 2008, I got put on
a Topps sport card.

Talking climbing with George Whitmore in El Cap Meadow at the 50th Anniversary of the Nose ascent, held in November 2008. Whitmore, along with Wayne
Merry, was part of Warren Harding's first ascent team. KEVIN POWELL

Alex and I pass a party mid pitch, in between Texas Flake and Boot Flake, during one of our test climbs in the fall of 2011. TOM EVANS

Psyche is high at "the finishing tree" after setting the speed record on the Nose with Alex Honnold in 2012. PAUL HARA

The minimal gear that Alex Honnold and I took up on our record speed ascent.

El Capitan is just a short walk through the woods from the street. Starting my 100th Nose ascent with Jayme Moye and Fiona Thornewill. STEVE ROKKS

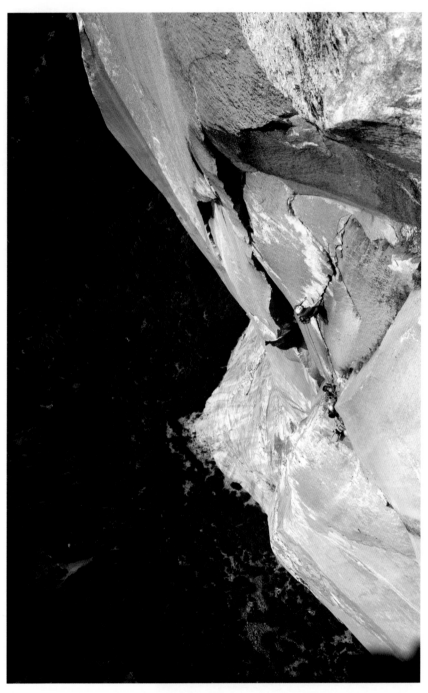

Climbing the 5.10c crack on pitch 30, with my partners (and the pig) below on the ledge known as "the wild stance." WILL MASTERMAN

An action shot of me on the King Swing during my 100th Nose Ascent, as Jayme and Fiona look on from the top of Boot Flake. STEVE ROKKS

Standing at the top of the Nose with Jayme Moye and Fiona Thornewill after making my 100th ascent.
STEVE ROKKS

My daughter Mari and me climbing the Nose in 2015.
WILL MASTERMAN

Marc Heileman and me standing on Texas Flake during my 101st ascent.

We didn't talk free climbing again until we reached Camp VI, the ledge at the top of pitch 26. Just ahead was a section known as "Changing Corners," another free-climbing conundrum. The walls of this flaring corner system are completely smooth, with a barely discernable crack running through the center. "I may need a little time to scope it out when I get up there," Lynn said.

I jokingly checked my watch. "Remember, time is of the essence," I said. Lynn shot me a wry smile. We were making good time and she knew it. Barring an unforeseen catastrophe, we would easily best mine and Nancy's time of 10:05.

Lynn didn't keep me waiting long. When she reached the anchor, she told me she'd paused to identify an alternate route that Brooke had created, which went up a steep face to the left of the original line, then back over to the right across a blank section of rock. "I don't know if it's going to work for me," she said, "it looks really reachy"—climber speak for requiring a long reach to move from handhold to handhold. Like her fingers, Lynn's wingspan was smaller than most, and in this instance, her size would work against her.

We topped out in 8 hours and 40 minutes. I was thrilled to have set a new male-female speed record. Lynn giggled at my elation. She seemed satisfied with her reconnaissance and full of praise for the Nose. "I'd nearly forgotten how beautiful it is," she said. "It's like it was sculpted by an artist or an angel."

I couldn't argue with that. My climb with Lynn marked my eighth ascent, and the Nose just kept getting better.

——————

With so much happening in Yosemite, I hadn't been back to Europe for the 1992 competition season yet. Then I got an offer I couldn't refuse: An invitation to compete at Rock Master. The annual competition held in Arco, Italy, dated back to 1987. It had since become the Wimbledon of rock climbing—an invitation-only event with the most prestige and prize money of any climbing comp on the planet. I was pretty sure I scored the invitation due to winning the World Championships in Speed in Frankfurt the year prior. Whatever the reason, I bought a plane ticket and went.

I was still undefeated in speed climbing and figured my chances of winning were pretty high. Plus, I'd heard nothing but good things about Arco, a charming town with more than a dozen climbing areas. When I arrived at the competition, I was pleased to find that the artificial wall had been erected outside, at the base of Colodri mountain, which I thought was very cool. I was displeased to hear that the promoters always used the same route, which meant Jacky Godoffe and all the other returning competitors knew it well.

I lost to Jacky in the finals round by less than half a second. I was seriously bummed until the awards ceremony, when I found out I'd won three million Italian lira, or US$1,722, for second place. That was half a year's expenses for me. Losing had never felt so good.

Christmas 1992 was tough for me and my family with my dad being gone. He and I had this goofy tradition where I'd buy him a gift of something I wanted for myself, and vice versa. The Christmas before the one when he'd gotten sick, I'd bought him a #4 Friend (he didn't climb), and he'd gotten me *Fifty Classic Climbs of North America* (I hadn't read much since college). The tome still resided at my parents' house in the family-room library.

I didn't go so far as to pick up the book and start reading it that Christmas, but seeing it again sparked an idea. In Europe "enchainments," an Anglicization of the French word *enchaînement*, meaning "linking," were getting a lot of media attention. Similar to what Peter Croft had been doing in Yosemite, mountaineers would link together two or more mountains in the Alps, or two or more routes on the same mountain, in one outing. So why not do an American version, a "Fifty Classic Climbs in Fifty Days" adventure? It could be my new project for 1993.

I mentioned the idea to Shipoopi, and he had a good laugh: "Hans, have you ever even opened that book?"

I had, but only to see the section on the Nose. Shipoopi told me that some of the climbs—like Hummingbird Ridge on Canada's Mount Logan—have never been repeated. Okay, so what about twenty-five classic climbs in twenty-five days? "Maybe," Shipoopi said. That was good enough for me. I drove to my mom's house to retrieve the book and started planning.

Besides Shipoopi, I invited Nancy and a local climber named Christian Santelices, whom I'd gotten friendly with at City Rock climbing gym. I pared down the fifty climbs to twenty that could logically be linked together in a twenty-day road trip through California, Utah, Colorado, and Wyoming. The "20 in 20" project would kick off Saturday, July 17, in Yosemite.

In the months I spent training for the adventure, Nancy and I broke up, and then Shipoopi busted his ankle after a bad paragliding landing. But I was set on making 20 in 20 happen. Once I get fixated on something, it's really hard for me to let it go.

Nancy and I weren't exactly on bad terms, so we decided to stay teammates for the sake of the project. Christian recommended his buddy Guillermo "Willie" Benegas, an Argentinean climber who'd just founded Benegas Brothers Expeditions with his twin brother, Damian, to replace Shipoopi. Willie turned out to be a good choice. He went on to become a famous mountaineer, racking up more than fifty ascents of Aconcagua, the highest mountain in South America, eleven ascents of Mount Everest, and eighty ascents of El Capitan (a man after my own heart).

In retrospect, 20 in 20 was a bigger achievement than our four collective experiences should have been able to accomplish at that stage in the game. But we were blissfully ignorant of that fact, or at least I was. I met the team in Yosemite, with a handwritten schedule of the climbs, like it was just another weekend climbing trip. We kicked off the project by climbing six classics inside Yosemite National Park in five days: Northwest Face of Half Dome, East Buttress on Middle Cathedral Rock, Steck-Salathé on Sentinel Rock, Royal Arches, Lost Arrow Spire, and, of course, the Nose on El Cap.

Based on previous climbing experience, it made sense to pair me with Nancy and Christian with Willie. Gearing up to climb the Nose with Nancy brought up a bittersweet nostalgia for the first time we'd climbed it together, back when we were just starting out as a couple, all shiny and happy and new. It could have been a bummer moment for me, but pretty much as soon as we started the route, I felt better. That's the thing about the Nose: It's always possible to have a good time on it, even with your ex-girlfriend. We cranked it out in 9:52.

After Yosemite we took to the road in my van, hitting a few of the alpine classics in the high Sierras; Castleton Tower in the Utah desert; a few of Colorado's classics, including the Diamond on Longs Peak; and wrapping it up with Wyoming's icons—Devil's Tower, the Tetons, and the Cirque of the Towers. After twenty days we had driven 69 hours, hiked 137 miles, canoed 2.5 hours, and climbed 241 pitches ranging from 5.5 to 5.13, for a total elevation gain of 60,080 feet. It was the greatest adventure of my life and, so far, has never been repeated.

Afterward, I returned to the Bay Area to address some nagging knee pain and ended up having surgery to remove a tear in my meniscus—the crescent-shaped piece of cartilage between the knee joints. During my recovery time on my mom's couch, I decided to step up my role with the American Sport Climbers Federation (now USA Climbing), the national governing body of competition climbing in the United States. I'd been on the board for two years, helping to grow the sport in the United States. They were looking for a new executive director to increase the local, regional, and national competitions, create a juniors organization, and build a national ranking system to track the best climbers. I felt like I was up for the challenge.

My interest wasn't purely altruistic; I was looking down the road. At age 29 I knew I couldn't climb this hard forever. At some point I'd be looking for a real job, most likely something in the climbing industry. I saw serving as executive director of the ASCF as a good résumé booster.

I also spent a fair amount of couch time thinking about my first post-surgery climb. If I went with the Nose, it would be my tenth ascent, which seemed like a meaningful get-back-on-the-horse climb. Plus, I still had something left to try on the Nose: to climb it by myself, solo, or what's known as "roped soloing."

Tom Bauman made the first roped-solo ascent of the Nose in 1969, and it was allegedly a grueling multiday endeavor. It took another twenty years for someone to do it in a day—in 1989 Shipoopi rope-soloed the Nose in 21 hours and 22 minutes. I'd never soloed anything before but was pretty sure that I was engineering-minded enough to figure it out. The question was more how long it would take. In retrospect, using the Nose as my sandbox to learn roped soloing probably wasn't the brightest idea I'd ever had. But at the time, it seemed like a grand adventure.

Shipoopi explained the basics and even drew me a diagram. I'd use a Grigri, much as I had when I simul-climbed with Peter Croft. The most important detail to remember was that I needed to build a multidirectional anchor to secure my rope to the *bottom* of the first pitch.

Exactly ten days (the doctor's recommendation for how long I should wait to walk again) after my knee surgery, I drove from my mom's house to Yosemite, camped in my van, and woke up early to attempt my tenth ascent of the Nose, this time alone. I didn't tell anyone that I had arrived in Yosemite, let alone that I was climbing the Nose solo. Keeping a low profile was not my usual style—they don't call me Hollywood Hans for nothing. But this climb was somehow different. I walked to the base by myself, enjoying the solitude and serenity of twilight.

At the start of pitch 1, I flaked out the rope and slotted it into the Grigri that was clipped to my harness. I studied the crack that leads up the first pitch and identified a good spot near the bottom, then built a bombproof multidirectional anchor and attached my rope. I checked my watch: 5:21 a.m. Time to climb.

I followed the crack upward, mostly free-climbing, using my hands and feet to work my way up, leaving the slower aid climbing for the harder sections. After the first 20 or so feet, I paused to insert protection, pulling a piece of pro from my harness and inserting it into the crack at waist height, then clipping in my rope. Shortly after, I felt a downward tug—the rope wasn't feeding smoothly through the Grigri. I stopped to put in another piece of pro and assessed the situation. Rope drag appeared to be the issue. I coiled up about 30 feet worth, letting it hang on the brake-end side of the rope, and clipped it into my harness. Problem solved.

I worked my way up the remaining 100 feet of the crack with a certain degree of caution. With the extra section of rope clipped up into my harness, I now had four lines dangling from me. Each time I went to clip my rope in for protection, I paused to make sure I was selecting the right one—the one coming out of the "climber" end of the Grigri. The others were just there for organizational purposes and would do little or nothing to arrest a fall.

When I reached the bolts at the top of pitch 1, I anchored in, finding it somewhat comical that my next step was to lower back down to the start. But so it goes with solo climbing—you need to go down to retrieve, or "clean," the pro you inserted into the wall on the way up. In regular partner climbing, the follower does that. In roped soloing you're the leader *and* the follower.

I switched out the Grigri, feeding the rope through in the opposite direction to convert it from a belay device to a rappel device, and lowered down. At the bottom I undid the anchor, clipping the cams back onto my harness, and then attached my ascenders to the rope to jug back up. As I worked I chuckled at myself for wearing my backpack when I initially climbed pitch 1. I could have left it at the bottom and saved myself the extra weight. Same with the ascenders. Oh well, I was figuring out best practices as I went.

I jugged up the rope with a bit more fire in my belly than usual to make up time lost on rookie mistakes. At the top I anchored in and checked my watch. 5:47 a.m. Not too shabby. I'd climbed pitch 1 twice and rappelled it once in 26 minutes.

Halfway up the second pitch, I hit my first real challenge: How do I do a pendulum without a partner belaying me? I anchored into the bolts that mark the spot to pendulum with my brain buzzing. I knew enough to thread the rope through the bolts and lower myself down using the Grigri. But then, once I'd swung over to the right, I didn't quite have enough rope to reach the crack and missed it, swinging back left.

If I'd had a partner, I would have yelled, "a little more," referring to slack. Since it was just me, I had to do it all myself. I released the brake device on the Grigri to give myself more slack and then swung over a second time. This time I grabbed the crack, but barely. I realized that without a partner, it was impossible to finesse the perfect amount of tension in the rope and that I'd just have to make do. With one hand on the crack, I grabbed the Grigri with the other to let out a bit more rope, then flung that hand back to the crack just before I peeled off. I hurried to jam a foot in, and once I felt steady, paused to catch my breath. It hadn't been pretty, but I'd successfully moved from one crack to another.

My next sticking point was at the base of pitch 7, a much larger pendulum. I thought it through and developed what initially seemed like a smart plan. I could clip one end of the rope into the bolts and swing over to the next crack. Then, since I had 60 meters (180 feet) worth of rope at my disposal, I could link pitches 7 and 8 together, thus only having to rappel once to clean the two pitches.

The theory was solid. In practice I ran into issues. Once I'd rapped down from the anchor atop pitch 8, I realized I needed to swing back over—reversing the pendulum—to unclip the rope from the base of pitch 7. But I didn't have the tail end of the rope to lower myself over there. So instead, I had to pull myself sideways across the wall, a grueling effort known as "traversing under tension."

Later, working my way up the Stove Leg crack, my mind churned through ideas for how I could have navigated that section better. I realized how much I was enjoying the problem-solving element of roped soloing and the opportunity for yet another flavor of adventure on the Nose. The one downer was my knee. It felt noticeably weaker.

Inside the chimney behind Texas Flake, my knee went from noticeably weaker to incredibly uncomfortable. I had my back pressed against one side of the chimney and my knees against the other, inching my way up. I had one of those "What the hell was I thinking?" moments as searing pain shot though my kneecap. I didn't even have any anti-inflammatories on me. There wasn't much I could do at that point except to keep going.

By the time I reached the King Swing, my knee was swollen. But I'd worked out the ideal pendulum sequence in my head. Or so I hoped.

Standing on top of Boot Flake, I threaded the rope through the bolts and tied one end into my harness. I slotted the other end into the Grigri. I had all my gear on me, including the backpack and ascenders. I wasn't planning on coming back. The way I'd figured it out, there would be nothing to clean.

I took a deep breath, then stepped off the flake, sitting back in my harness with my feet on the wall. I opened the brake lever on the Grigri to lower myself down the entire length of the 60-foot boot, and then another 30 or so feet below that. Suspended about 1,500 feet above the ground, I glanced around to be sure I'd lowered to precisely the right spot for the swing. Feeling satisfied with my position, I went for it. I ran sideways to the right, along the smooth granite beneath Boot Flake, to get some extra momentum, and then ran left, swinging over to grab hold of the arête and bear-crawling sideways to the next crack system. That was the easy part.

Above me loomed about 100 feet worth of crack. It wasn't too difficult of a climb, rated 5.10. What was sketchy was my protection—my rope was attached to the bolts atop Boot Flake some 100 feet above and 40 feet over to the right. If I slipped and fell, I'd get yanked to the right into what would essentially be a very messy reverse King Swing. The odds of me falling neatly and upright were slim. I would more likely be flailing, possibly inverted, and in serious danger of injury by granite collision.

I moved carefully up the crack, my mind razor-sharp with the knowledge that a slip would pretty much mean the end of my solo attempt. It was a relief to reach the top of the pitch. But there was still one more test to determine if I'd chosen the best method. I anchored into the bolts and untied the rope from my harness. Then, for the moment of truth, I began hauling the rope. I held my breath as the tail swung out to Boot Flake and cleanly pulled through the bolts. Ha! I'd done it—soloed the biggest pendulum on the Nose, without having to go back and clean even a single piece of gear.

My elation didn't last long. Climbing the next section, the Grey Bands, is a bit of a pain no matter what you do, because it's more of a traverse than a climb. I was basically roped-soloing sideways, building an anchor on the right-hand side of the pitch, lead-climbing over to the left-hand side, "rapping" back to the right where I'd started, and then jugging my way back to the left to clean the gear. It was tedious, to say the least. And about to get worse.

I was at the end of the last pitch before the Great Roof, cleaning the final pieces of gear as I jugged my way up on ascenders, when I felt a tug on the rope—the type of tug that can only mean one thing. It was stuck. In my nine times on the Nose, I'd learned that the Grey Bands were notorious for snagging ropes. But it seemed like a terrible injustice to make it almost all the way through the Nose's worst rope-eating terrain only to get stuck just beneath the bolts at the top of the last pitch.

Maybe it wasn't as bad as it seemed. I grasped one end of the rope and gave it a slow, firm tug. Nothing. Then I did the same to the other. Still nothing. I shook the rope, just in case I could dislodge it. No luck. I anchored into the bolts with a sigh, removed my backpack, and set up to rappel. Adding insult to injury, I'd linked pitches 20 and 21 together. Had the climb gone smoothly, linking the pitches would have been more efficient, but in this case, it meant I had to go twice as far back down to rescue the rope.

The culprit turned out to be the jagged edge of a small flake. The rope had presumably gotten caught there and then worked itself into the crack behind the flake. I pried it out and put my ascenders on to jug back up. In the moment, the episode felt like a huge waste of time. In reality, I only lost about 5 minutes. I've since come to understand that the Nose throws out all kinds of challenges, big and small. And dealing with them is, well, character building in its own little way. Plus, in the realm of NIAD, losing a couple minutes to rope maintenance doesn't make much of a difference in the end. It's certainly not worth any gnashing of teeth.

I was actually making really good time. Shipoopi had rope-soloed the Nose in under 22 hours, which I was using as an approximate gauge. To that effect, I was aiming to make it to the Great Roof, which is just past the halfway point, in 12 hours. Even with the rope getting stuck, I got there in eight.

I began the second half of the route feeling smoother and considerably more confident about roped-solo technique. And not a moment too soon—as I approached the bivi ledge known as Camp V, I encountered another party. The three men were thunderstruck that it was just me, myself, and I.

"We've spotted you a couple other times on the wall behind us and have been trying to figure out what the heck you were doing," said one.

"And how the heck you were doing it," said his friend.

"Well, remember, I'm not hauling a pig," I told them.

"Still," said climber no. 1.

They were happy to let me pass, and I was happy to give a demonstration. They watched as I built my anchor at the base of the next pitch. It occurred to me that I was having a different experience on the Nose than they were, and it suited me well: climbing very long granite routes very efficiently, very light, and very fast.

I reached the last pitch about 7 hours faster than Shipoopi must have, and after making my way up to nearly the top of the final bolt ladder, I did something unusual—I paused. Not because I had to figure out a better method or unsnag a rope or catch my breath. I stopped because I wanted to take it all in. I was about to top out on the Nose for the tenth time, something very few others had accomplished. And I had done it solo, in less than 24 hours, previously an exclusive club of one: Shipoopi. But more than any of that, I stopped because it was just so damn colossal.

In the soft light of early evening, I could see the entire route spread beneath me, the silver granite sweeping out to meet the forest where I'd started. I glanced down at the upper dihedrals, the Grey Bands, the top of Dolt Tower, the Stove Legs, and then spotted a climber on Sickle Ledge, appearing as a dot, a single pixel on the canvas of El Capitan.

I topped out at 7:32 p.m., setting a roped-solo record of 14:11. My knee had swollen to the size of a small volleyball, but I felt very little pain. As I started the hike back to the bottom, I thought back on my first failed attempt with Mike Lopez the year I'd graduated college and had a chuckle. I felt a lot of gratitude that Mike had given the climb another shot with me, and for all the partners I'd had since. But at the same time, I felt a deep satisfaction that, this time, it had been just me and the Nose.

The next month, September, Lynn Hill succeeded in making the first free ascent of the Nose. It took her and climbing partner Brooke Sandahl four days and three nights on the wall. Lynn had no problem with Jardine's Traverse or the Great Roof. Her sticking point ended up being Changing Corners, but she worked it out, following the original line instead of Brooke's "reachy" variation. Today, Changing Corners is considered the free-climbing crux of the Nose, giving the route a rating of 5.14a. To date, only four others—Scotty Burke, Beth Rodden, Tommy Caldwell, and Jorg Verhoeven—have free-climbed the Nose. It remains one of the hardest free climbs of its size in the world.

With all of the big adventure news happening on the Nose—from seemingly unbreakable new speed records to the first all-free ascent—it was hard to imagine that the best was still yet to come.

CHAPTER 6

Blind Ambition

In 1994, the year following my roped-solo ascent of the Nose, the Access Fund, an advocacy organization focused on conserving climbing areas in the United States, auctioned off a "Climb the Nose with Steve Schneider and Hans Florine" expedition as part of their annual fund-raising dinner. Two really cool guys in their late 20s, Craig Cleveland and Jim Soash, donated a couple thousand dollars for the "privilege." But really, I was the one who felt privileged. People were starting to associate me with the Nose, and I couldn't think of a bigger honor in the world of big-wall climbing.

Meanwhile, it was sport climbing that paid my meager living expenses. On US soil I remained undefeated in speed. In 1995 I got invited to the first-ever X Games, held in Newport, Rhode Island. Part competition, part festival, the event spanned a full week and was the brainchild of sports-broadcasting network ESPN. It focused exclusively on "extreme sports," which included in-line skating, skateboarding, BMX biking, mountain biking, street luge, bungee jumping, water-ski jumping, and rock climbing. I won Speed the inaugural year (as well as in 1996 and 1997), earning $1,000 and an offer from Steve West at Boreal to pay me for doing climbing slideshows.

Five years after leaving Parker Seals, I was still living out of my '76 GMC van and generally enjoying life on the road. I traveled from popular sport-climbing cliffs like Rifle in Colorado to local climbing competitions like Phil's Backyard Cave Comp, to the big national competitions in Seattle and North Conway. Following the sport-climbing scene—and reuniting with the same folks every few weeks at the crags and comps—made for a fun lifestyle.

Still, the projects I looked forward to the most were the ones on the big walls of Yosemite. For whatever reason, I thoroughly enjoyed covering huge amounts of granite in one push. And I was starting to get good at it. In June 1994 I succeeded in my first linkup "in a day": Shipoopi and I climbed the Nose followed by the Steck-Salathé on Sentinel Rock in less than 24 hours. We also completed "the El Cap Trifecta," climbing three routes on the big stone, including the Nose, in a day. Plus, I nabbed my fifth ascent of the Salathé, which had become my second-favorite route on El Cap after the Nose, and set a new speed record, with Shipoopi, on Lurking Fear, a nineteen-pitch, 2,000-foot route to the far left of the Nose, in 8:52.

As for the Nose, there suddenly seemed to be an endless supply of colorful characters who wanted to take a run up El Cap's original line with me. Besides Access Fund bidders, I climbed the Nose with old friends from the comp scene, new friends from the climbing gym, my brother Neal, and even a caver from Puerto Rico by the name of Rossano Boscarino, who held two world records in "mechanical vertical rope climbing." But my most unforgettable ascent in the mid-1990s was with Erik Weihenmayer.

In April 1996 I went to the Phoenix Bouldering contest for the tenth year in a row. The oldest climbing competition in the United States, the event had begun to feel a bit like a family reunion. Shipoopi was excited to introduce me to Erik, an up-and-coming climber he'd met a few days earlier while giving a slideshow presentation elsewhere in Arizona.

"He's amazing," Shipoopi said. "Totally one of a kind."

Erik Weihenmayer was working on a bouldering problem on the Piranha Wall when we approached. At the Phoenix Bouldering Comp, you're not allowed to take beta from other climbers. In other words, you can't have a friend standing there coaching you on the route. Yet, that's exactly what Erik was doing. "Big reach with the right hand," said Erik's buddy. "Farther, farther . . . that's the one."

I watched as the tall, muscular climber latched onto the hold with a bloody hand and taped-up finger. He moved a bit more slowly than most, his every move guided by the voice of his friend. I looked around, and no one else seemed concerned that they were breaking the rules. As I watched, I began to notice that much of what the friend said seemed obvious, like "cactus on your left, keep it tight." That's when it hit me—Erik Weihenmayer couldn't see.

I turned to Shipoopi with a questioning look. "Yeah, man," he said. "The dude's completely blind."

We watched Erik until he'd finish the climb, and then Shipoopi introduced us. I'm pretty sure my jaw was still on the ground. Erik grasped my hand and shook it enthusiastically, a huge grin on his face. He told me that he loved climbing and hoped to climb the Seven Summits. He'd already done Denali, a nineteen-day effort, the year prior. Erik worked as a middle school teacher at Phoenix Country Day School and was hoping to spend some time training in Yosemite over summer break.

"I need to know your honest opinion," he said. "Can a blind guy climb the Nose?"

"Absolutely," I said.

In retrospect, maybe I should have hesitated. The only adaptive climber I knew of was Mark Wellman, who was paralyzed from the waist down and climbed El Cap via a route known as the Shield in 1989. The endeavor took him eight days. I'd never heard of a blind person who could climb, let alone one who'd attempted the Nose.

Two months later Erik showed up in Yosemite Valley with climbing partners Jeff Evans and Sam Bridgem and rented a house in Yosemite West. That summer I spent a fair amount of time hanging out and climbing with them. I learned that Erik wasn't born blind, but his vision rapidly deteriorated due to a rare condition known as juvenile retinoschisis. By the time he entered high school, the disorder had completely robbed him of his sight. Erik said he was really angry and fought hard against leaving the sighted world behind, refusing to use a cane or learn Braille.

Thankfully, he got into wrestling as a freshman, which helped satisfy his natural athleticism and provided a healthy outlet for his many frustrations. Then, in his later teen years, Erik got into rock climbing. The tactile nature of the sport made it a surprisingly good fit.

One morning in July I took Erik, Jeff, and Sam to Leaning Tower, an overhanging granite cliff located downstream from El Capitan, to practice big-wall climbing techniques like jugging, hauling the pig, and overnight bivying. I chose Leaning Tower because it's the perfect length, about 700 feet, to do in two days and one night. The wall tips out at about 110 degrees, which makes towing the pig less of a hassle. The slight overhang also makes it safer to fall, and I wanted to assess Erik's lead-climbing skills.

I quickly saw that Erik was unusually strong at jugging. His upper body strength was most likely born of necessity. Since he couldn't use his eyes to scan for holds, he'd lock off one arm and feel around with his opposite hand, building a level of strength and endurance that other first-time big-wall climbers didn't possess. With ascenders in hand, he was a monster—zipping up the rope in perfect rhythm, no eyesight needed.

Erik wasn't nearly as comfortable lead climbing. He took a stab at leading the last pitch but bailed after about 15 feet. I realized that without vision, he had no idea what gear was on his rack, except by feel. I watched him expend precious time and energy feeling his way through his rack to find the right piece. And then, once he got a piece of pro in, he had to take his hand off the trigger and feel the edges of the cam to make sure he'd selected the right size. The entire time, he was laboriously hanging off the wall with just one arm.

I filed away these observations for the Nose. Lying in my van on the nights leading up to our August 6 attempt, I found myself going through the climb pitch by pitch, looking for ways to not only maximize Erik's strengths but also improve his efficiency—like his rack. What if we organized it by type and size? Stoppers, smallest to biggest on his right gear loop. Cams, smallest to biggest on his left. Anything else, like ascenders and aiders, could go on the back loops. Heck, that seemed like a good practice for all of us. Some people may have thought it was crazy to climb the Nose with a blind guy, but I absolutely couldn't wait. It was a challenge unlike any I'd ever known.

The day before the climb, I created a precise schedule for day 1:

4:15	*Leave cabin*
5:32	*Arrive at El Cap Meadow + begin hike to base*
5:56	*Reach base*
6:07	*Finish organizing gear*
6:22	*Last climber off the ground*
10:37	*Arrive at Sickle Ledge*

I'd been scheduling my life using "exacting times" since college. It was my way of making every minute count. But I rarely shared that fact with others outside of my family and best friends. I hadn't known Erik all that long, but something told me he'd appreciate the quirk. I handed over the schedule to the team. Jeff read it out loud and I watched Erik's pursed lips spread into his big, goofy grin. "Hans, you're something else," he said laughing.

97

According to my plan, we would climb the Nose in four days and three nights. On the first day we'd be close enough to the ground—about 500 feet on Sickle Ledge—to set fixed lines and rappel down to the base and sleep in our own beds that night. On day 2 we'd jug the fixed lines back to Sickle Ledge and proceed from there. Day 1 wasn't exactly a full day of climbing, more like getting a head start and a way to ease everyone into what would be a difficult, yet hopefully satisfying, expedition.

On the hike to the base, I shared how we'd divide up the work on day 1. There are four pitches to Sickle Ledge, and with a four-man team, we'd each take one. I assigned Erik pitch 2. I wanted him to have the experience of doing one of the Nose's iconic pendulums, and the second pitch would be the safest option for someone who'd literally be flying blind.

When it was Erik's turn, I belayed him as he climbed steadily up the thin, 40-foot crack leading to the pendulum point. I knew from his two months in the valley that he was a solid crack climber. Erik could readily feel his way up the crack without sight. As he'd told me during one of our practice climbs: With cracks, there are no hidden holds lurking just out of reach, no way to accidentally wander off route.

"You're there," I called up when he'd nearly reached the pendulum point. I watched him feel for the bolts and clip in. "This is it," I said to Jeff and Sam, who were standing with me on the small ledge at the base of pitch 2.

"Okay, I'm going to lower you down about 10 feet and then you're going to pendulum to the right and grab for the crack," I yelled up to Erik.

"How far?" Erik called down.

"As far as the rope will let you," I said

The three of us watched as Erik jogged across the wall to the right. But before he could get a hand on the crack, he hit the end of the rope and swung back left. "More momentum," I yelled up to him. "The crack's there—you need to commit."

This time, Erik jogged to the left to get a running start and then ran right. The pendulum took effect, and he arced upward. "Now," I yelled. Eric's hand slapped the crack, but he didn't quite catch the edge and he swung back.

"Third time's a charm," I called up.

"Right," Erik grunted. He waited until he'd stopped swinging, took a deep breath, and tried again. This time his hand hit the jagged edge of the crack and clamped down. He'd stuck it.

"That's the one," I called up, and Erik began moving up the crack.

"So awesome," Jeff said in a hushed voice.

Later that day, after we'd descended from Sickle Ledge, we walked over to El Cap Meadow and took a dip in the Merced River. Even on the hottest August day, the water stays cool enough to feel incredibly refreshing. Once we were all submerged, I gave the team the good news. "Guys," I said. "I think we're going to make it."

Day 2 began with all of us jugging the fixed lines back up to Sickle Ledge, and this time we had the pig in tow. We had two pigs actually— with four guys spending three days and two nights on the wall, I'd needed to add a second, smaller haul bag. The "mini pig" contained all the canned food we'd eat for dinner, three of the twelve gallons of water, and one person's sleeping gear. It weighed about 40 pounds.

Instead of hauling the pigs pitch by pitch up to Sickle Ledge, I decided to use a method I'd figured out earlier in the season while leading other small groups up the Nose: I'd attach the pig to my harness and tow it up with me. The extra 70 pounds turns an otherwise mundane stretch of jugging into a great workout.

I clipped one end of a lanyard to the pig, and the other end to my harness. Jeff and Sam looked at me like I was crazy. "Hans is making like a pack mule," Sam told Erik.

"Yeah, and you're next," I said to Erik. "There are two pigs—let's put all that strength of yours to good use." I clipped the mini-pig to the back of Erik's harness.

"What the heck?" Erik asked.

"Just do your thing," I told him. Erik started jugging and then groaned when he got high enough off the ground to feel the extra weight of the pig. But he was smiling at the same time. I knew Erik well enough by that point to know he didn't want to be the token blind climber. He was happy to be taking one for the team. He and I jugged up to Sickle Ledge side by side, collectively complaining about our pigs.

The day 2 plan was to progress from Sickle Ledge to El Cap Tower—ten pitches—and spend the night on El Cap Tower. I assigned Erik the Stove Leg crack for his pitch. He already knew the story of the name, having heard it straight from Warren Harding himself upon meeting the old codger in Yosemite a few weeks prior. Erik was a bit of a climbing-history buff and seemed pleased to be tasked with such an infamous crack.

Before sending him off, I double-checked that Erik had a rack full of #2 cams. The piece is a necessity for ascending the roughly 2-inch-wide crack, or "granite lips," as Erik called it.

Erik stepped up into the crack to begin his ascent. I watched him methodically free-climb it, stuffing one foot and both sets of fingers into the crack, torquing them so they held, standing up on his foot and then jamming the other foot into the crack above it. Every 15 feet or so, he'd stop to insert a #2 cam for protection and clip his rope into it. At times, he'd attach an aider to the piece of pro, step into the webbing ladder, and rest. On some sections he appeared to be moving easily, gracefully. On others he struggled, grunting and shaking from the effort. In all those ways, he was no different from any other climber.

The difference is that Erik is missing a piece of gear that makes every-thing easier: eyesight. Every time he put a piece of protection into the wall, he had to feel the edges of the cam to make sure he'd selected the right size. This ate up energy and caused him to move more slowly than others with the same level of experience in big-wall climbing would have. It also scared the hell out of me to watch him. In my head I berated myself for putting him in such a difficult situation. At the same time, I knew Erik wouldn't have wanted it any other way.

It was 6 p.m. when we reached Dolt Tower—the seventh of the ten pitches I'd scheduled for the day. I ran some numbers in my head: We'd been climbing for 11 hours. Moving at our current rate of about 1.5 hours per pitch, we'd need another 4.5 hours to reach El Cap Tower, where I'd planned for us to spend the night. We also needed to eat dinner. "Guys, we're calling it a day here," I announced.

I secured the pigs at the anchor on one end of the ledge atop Dolt Tower, and then fixed a rope horizontally so we could clip in while still having the freedom to move back and forth across the ledge. Because there were four of us, I set up a portaledge, which sleeps two. The other two would sleep on the rock ledge.

We were all starving by then. I tore into the food, handing out spoons and cans of soup. "You get your can for 1 minute, then pass to the left," I instructed. "Ready, go." I kept my eye on the watch and after 60 seconds called out "switch!" We made it through four rounds of musical cans before they were all empty.

None of us moved after dinner. We just sat in a row on the ledge, backs against the wall, legs straight out in front of us, soaking in the view. Erik explained how he could "sense" the height without being able to see how high we were off the ground, kind of like the way I could feel all the open space around me while climbing in the dark.

As the sun started to set, I saw lights in El Cap Meadow, some 1,000 feet below. Not headlights or flashlights but glow sticks, spinning and arcing. "Looks like we're getting a laser light show," I said.

Erik laughed. "That's my girlfriend, Ellen, and my dad. They told me they were going to try that."

I listened as Sam described for Erik in vivid detail every move the lights made. We gave our applause by flicking our headlamps on and off and yelling at the top of our lungs.

The sky was clear and dark, exposing a million twinkling stars that evening. Before we drifted off to sleep, Erik told me that his dad was his biggest supporter, writing letters to sponsors, helping with logistics and fund-raising, and cheering from the sidelines. I smiled thinking of my own dad, who, before he died, had done pretty much the same. I learned that Erik too had lost a parent. His mom died tragically in a car accident when he was 16.

Along with the rising sun on the morning of day 3, I also felt an increased sense of urgency. We were starting the day already four pitches behind and then had twelve more on top of that to make it to Camp VI, where we'd sleep. To save time, I made the executive decision to take over leading, at least until we got back on schedule. I broke the news to the rest of the team over breakfast. Their reaction was cooperative. "Whatever we need to do," Jeff said.

I knew that regardless of whether the team was climbing or jugging, they wouldn't be disappointed by the day's features. We moved through some of the route's most thrilling terrain, including Texas and Boot Flake (and the super-exposed "granite sea" between them), the King Swing, the Grey Bands, and the Great Roof. It was an absolute blast for me to watch their reactions.

When we reached the Great Roof, it was Erik's turn to be the follower, which meant he was the team member responsible for cleaning my pro. The other two would simply be jugging. I hesitated for a moment, because the 30-foot traverse directly beneath the roof is probably the sketchiest place to clean on the entire 3,000-foot route. There are no hand- or footholds, just smooth granite. And to extract the pro from the seam between the overhanging roof and the wall requires swinging from piece to piece, kind of like the monkey bars on the playground—if monkey bars were 2,000 feet high, anyway.

"The traverse directly under the roof isn't going to be easy," I told him.

"Hans, nothing is," Erik replied.

"All right, I'm going to be right there to coach you through it," I said.

I completed the lead and then anchored into the bolts just to the right of the roof, sitting back in my harness and watching Erik. When he reached the horizontal section directly beneath the overhang, he paused. "Okay, this is it," I told him. "You're going to need to unclip one of your ascenders."

"What?!" Erik said, more an exclamation than a question. The two ascenders are never removed from the rope. Besides serving as handholds, each has a stirrup dangling from it that serves as a foothold. The ascenders are the follower's only two points of contact.

"This section is the one place you'll ever need to do this," I said. "It's the only way to get the pro out beneath an overhang, when all your weight is on the rope."

I knew Erik was technical-minded enough to understand the technique and the rationale behind it. But I also knew that wouldn't make it any less terrifying. He was holding on to his ascenders, standing with both feet in the stirrups. I watched him let go with his right hand and feel for the pro and then the rope on the other side of it. Then he transferred all his weight to his left foot, unhooked the right-hand ascender from the rope, and reclamped it on the other side of the pro. He carefully put weight back on his right foot. Now he was straddling the pro.

Next he shifted all his weight onto his right foot and began working the pro out of the crack. It didn't come easy—none of the pieces under the Great Roof do. After several minutes I could see the frustration on his face. "Stay with it," I told him. "It takes a good amount of finessing."

When the piece finally came out, the rope came free like Tarzan's vine, swinging Erik a few feet over to the next piece. He let out a little yelp, a reaction to the falling sensation. I winced, hoping that the next piece held and he didn't have to endure a double swing. It did, thankfully. Erik jugged up to it and began the entire process again. He would repeat it eight times to clear the roof.

The technique wouldn't have been any different had Erik been sighted. But it may have been faster and it certainly would have been less scary. When he arrived at the anchor 25 minutes later, he was noticeably fatigued.

"Great work," I told him, and handed him my water bottle.

He managed a smile before gulping down water. I didn't say it out loud, because I didn't want to embarrass him, but I was pretty sure Erik Weihenmayer had the toughest mental game in town.

We ended up having to climb several hours in the dark to reach the sleeping ledge known as Camp VI. With the exception of Erik, we'd all donned headlamps. "Don't need one," he said wryly. We were back on schedule, but it had been a long, hard day. At Camp VI I fell asleep as soon as I laid down.

We woke up the next day with five pitches to go and almost no water left. Still, spirits were high. I assigned Erik to climb the last pitch—the steep overhanging bolt ladder. I knew he had the strength for it, plus the added incentive of his father and Ellen waiting at the top, alongside camera crews and local reporters who'd heard about "the blind guy" climbing the Nose.

We topped out after another full day of climbing, for a total of 4 days of effort. It was the first (and only) ascent where I've ever lost track of the exact time. Erik had just become the first blind person to climb the Nose. The seconds, minutes, and hours no longer mattered.

At the top Ellen and Erik embraced, and the reporters surrounded him. I stood off to the side, watching and smiling. Shipoopi, who had hiked up with the film crew as an assistant, came over and stood beside me. He spoke quietly, in a rare moment of seriousness: "I know how hard that was for you because I can see it."

At his words my eyes welled up with tears. I had been so inspired by Erik's strength of character and commitment to face his fears that I hadn't realized how utterly fatigued I was. I sat down and let the tears fall—a product of physical and mental exhaustion, and pride at having played a part in the incredible adventure that Erik had led us all on.

Erik has since climbed the Seven Summits, including, in 2001, becoming the first blind person to summit Everest. We'd rope up together again in 2006 for the first blind ascent of Mount Kenya, and then again in 2008 for 16,023-foot Carstensz Pyramid on the island of New Guinea, which many consider the "Eighth Summit." Erik's belief that you can do anything you set your mind to echoes my own life philosophy about human potential. Climbing El Cap was "impossible" until Warren Harding did it in 1958. Then it was impossible to climb it in a day until Bridwell et al. in 1975. And it was impossible for a blind person before Erik. By the time you read this, someone else who had been previously thought too old, too young, too busy (is that you?), or "too disabled" will have already climbed El Cap.

When I stood with Erik atop the Nose in 1996, I figured I'd pretty much experienced everything the Nose had to offer. As it turns out, I hadn't.

CHAPTER 7

Married with Children

In 1997 I decided I wanted to settle down in Yosemite—in something other than a van. I asked around to get a sense for real estate prices, and, sadly, the most I could afford was a small cabin about an hour outside the park. Perhaps with running water. Then my cell phone rang.

"Hello?"

"Hi Hans, it's Theresa at Mountain Travel Sobek."

I'd met Theresa the year prior when I'd climbed the Nose with Erik Weihenmayer. The company she worked for was based in Berkeley and had broadcast live feeds of the climb on the Internet, which was a novel concept at the time.

"I heard you were looking to buy a place in Yosemite?" she said. "My parents are actually thinking of selling."

I knew her parents' place: a beautiful three-story A-frame house located about a block from the one that Erik and his team had rented in Yosemite West—a residential section in the forested hills on the southern end of the park. Mountain Travel Sobek had thrown a small party there to celebrate Erik's ascent.

"Thanks Theresa," I'd told her. "But I can't afford anything inside the park, especially not your parents' place."

"It's not really about the money for them," she said. "They want some-one who loves the park to own it, not some speculator."

It sounded too good to be true. That house was worth at least a quar-ter million.

"Theresa," I said, "I *really* love the park. Let me see what kind of money I can pull together."

I hung up with her and called my mom, then my grandma, and cob-bled together a family loan for a down payment. Theresa's parents would end up selling me their place for maybe half of what it was worth. I moved in in August 1997, with a plan to rent it out as often as I could to pay back my family and cover my monthly mortgage payments. I was 33 years old and felt like I had everything I'd ever wanted in life.

Well, almost everything. My vagabond lifestyle hadn't exactly been conducive to long-term relationships. Shipoopi had gotten married three years prior, in 1994, and my older sister was already married with children. Getting married and having a family seemed like a bit of a pipe dream for this marginally successful professional climber. I wasn't even sure if I'd be able to make my monthly house payments.

Meanwhile, a new climber had begun to make his mark on Yosemite Valley. Dean Potter, a 25-year-old college dropout from New Hamp-shire, rope-soloed the Regular Northwest Face of Half Dome in a mind-bending 4 hours and 17 minutes, cutting the previous fastest solo, set by Steve Monks in 1980, in half. In the climbing world Half Dome is second only to El Capitan in lore, and its unusual shape—one-half of a gray granite dome that appears to have been perfectly sliced in two—makes it the most recognizable feature in Yosemite. Allegedly, Potter barely used his rope on the climb, scaling Half Dome's 2,000-foot granite face mostly unprotected. Not even Peter Croft had been so bold.

Potter went on a tear after that, partnering with other Yosemite up-and-comers including Jose Pereyra, Cedar Wright, Timmy O'Neill, and

Miles Smart to break many of the long-standing big-wall speed records in the park. Times were dropping faster than the climbing magazines could keep track. I started the website Speedclimb.com to track Yosemite big-wall records in real time.

It was an exciting time to be in the valley. I loved the energy. These guys were all younger than me, but that didn't stop me from throwing myself into the mix. Setting speed records on big walls combined two of my favorite things: covering large chunks of granite in one push and climbing fast.

In September 1998 Dean Potter and Jose Pereyra broke the speed record that Andy Puhvel and I had set on the Salathé in 1991 by 7 minutes. Later that month Shipoopi and I took it back, slicing another 41 minutes off, for a new record of 8:02. Also in September, Potter and Pereyra went after the record on the Regular Northwest Face of Half Dome, which Peter Coward and I held in a time of 3:01. They whittled it down to 2:56. The following year Jim Herson and I improved on it further, taking the time to 2:25 and then 1:53. Again in September Potter and Pereyra set a new record on Lurking Fear, besting the time Shipoopi and I had set in 1994 by an hour and 37 minutes. We responded in 2000, taking the time down by another hour and 53 minutes to 5:22.

The time differences were more due to efficiency and process improvements than they were to raw athleticism. One of my favorite examples is "Mitroviching." Steve Gerberding had made the first one-day ascent of Zodiac, a sixteen-pitch, 1,800-foot route on El Capitan, in 1993, in a time of 17:52. In 1999 a climber named Russ Mitrovich did it in 12 hours. With the exception of 10 feet of belayed free climbing at the base of a tricky section known as the White Circle, Mitrovich climbed the entire route sans rope, clipping daisy chains into various fixed gear placements for protection. It was brilliantly efficient and slightly crazy.

Off the wall, I didn't cross paths with any of these guys very often—they were living in their vans or hanging out at Camp 4, while I'd assumed a more gentlemanly lifestyle in Yosemite West. Occasionally, Potter and Pereyra would make an appearance on my back deck and party with the old guys. Potter's stories, in particular, made me smile. He had a natural flare for drama. He'd get busted for hard partying at Camp 4 by Yosemite's search and rescue team, never mind that he was part of the team.

—•—

On Memorial Day weekend in 1999, I stood on the front porch of my house waiting. My friend Maria had just pulled into the driveway with a car full of her climbing friends. I watched three men and three women unfold themselves out of the car and looked for the one Maria had described to me on the phone as the "supermodel turned alpinist." Not that Jacki was hard to spot. At just over 5 feet 10 inches tall, with shiny shoulder-length brown hair and green eyes, she possessed the type of beauty rarely seen outside the pages of fashion magazines and movie screens. I tried not to stare at her as I welcomed the group into my home.

"Okay, first things first," said Maria. "How did you go from living in a van to living here?"

"My massive contest winnings," I joked. "Speed climbing is a very lucrative career."

Maria laughed. "Seriously."

"It's a seriously amazing story," I said. Once we'd all settled into the expansive living room with floor-to-ceiling windows overlooking the woods beyond, I told Maria and her friends how I came to possess my dream home two years prior, then showed them around to their rooms.

I spent the next couple days climbing with Maria and her crew, learning what I could about Jacki. She'd worked for Ford Models in

Manhattan, appearing numerous times on the cover of *Vogue*, *Cosmopolitan*, and *Glamour*, among other magazines. She'd recently moved to Los Angeles to pursue her passion for acting. She'd learned to climb in the Gunks and held a New York State guide license. Since being out west, she'd taken to mountaineering, summiting the monster peaks of the Cascades, including Rainer and Shasta, and 14,505-foot Mount Whitney in the Sierras, the highest summit in the contiguous United States.

Jacki was smart and interesting and so damn beautiful. But she didn't seem interested in me. It wasn't until she shared her goal of becoming the first woman to solo the Nose that I thought I might have a chance. I had rope-soloed the Nose in 1993 and still held the record time of 14 hours and 11 minutes. When I told her, she laughed, a sweet, twinkling sound. "I'm planning to take my time," she said. "For me, it's the journey, not the destination."

Shot down.

On the group's last day, I found myself alone with Jacki at Elephant Rock. She told me that Peter, one of the other climbers in the group, was her ex-boyfriend, and out of respect for that, she'd refrained from showing any feelings for me. I stammered something awkward at best, utterly unintelligible at worst. Jacki continued. "I really like you," she said, looking straight into my eyes. "I'd like to get together another time when it's just the two of us."

She came back a month later. We climbed Eye in the Sky on Half Dome, a seven-pitch, 1,500-foot face climb rated 5.10d. Unlike the Nose on El Cap, which is an easy 15-minute hike from the car, Eye in the Sky has a 6-mile approach following a rugged trail through Yosemite's backcountry. Jacki and I talked the entire hike with Half Dome beckoning overhead like a Renaissance sculpture. We passed at least two incredible waterfalls on our way, but all I remember is the sound of her laughter. On the rock Jacki and I climbed as if we'd been climbing together all our lives, a natural, easy synergy.

The hike down from the top of Half Dome is an adventure in itself, with 6 miles through Half Dome's "death slabs." Jacki wasn't fazed by the steep slabs, the sudden drop-offs that required us to rappel, or use the hand-over-hand lines. I imagined it was a fitting first date for a super-model-turned-alpinist who appreciated the journey even more than the destination. Jacki must have thought so too, because by the end of the day, I had a new girlfriend.

What I didn't have was a decision on my next climbing project. I was ready for something big, something huge, actually, like a roped-solo linkup. Climbers had been rhapsodizing about the enchainment of Yosemite's two most iconic rock formations—El Capitan and Half Dome—for as long as I could remember, but so far, no one had tried it solo. I'd been seriously considering it for a couple of months. The emphasis on the challenge is completing the linkup in less than 24 hours. I had to be sure I could hit that mark. For climbers, rope-soloing a big wall "in a day" is like breaking the 2-hour marathon for runners. I knew others, including Dean Potter, were contemplating a solo attempt to link up the Nose on El Cap with the Regular Northwest Face of Half Dome. And I knew that whoever did it first would be well remembered in the history of Yosemite climbing.

After Jacki and I officially started dating, I decided to go for it. Maybe it's the old adage that behind every strong man is an even stronger woman. Or maybe doing the linkup was like my last hurrah before settling down in a serious relationship. At any rate, I wanted "accountability partners" for committing to this huge challenge, so once I made my decision, I told my friends that I was going to go for it. Then I made it official by posting an announcement on Speedclimb.com: I would attempt the linkup on July 24, 1999, under the light of a full moon.

I started with the Regular Northwest Face of Half Dome, making fantastic time in 3:57. This was the same route that had put Dean Potter on the map a year ago for his time of 4:17. I'd just shaved 20 minutes off that, setting a new record. I was feeling like Superman on my way to the Nose, where I ran into Shipoopi, who as it turned out, was looking to intercept me.

"3:57 on Half Dome!" I blurted out, ecstatic to tell my best friend. But he looked grim.

"Dude, Dean Potter's already done it," Shipoopi said.

"Yeah, but I just did it 20 minutes faster," I said.

"No, I mean the linkup, man. He did it yesterday."

"What?"

"He was in Colorado and jumped on a plane after he heard you were planning to go for it."

I stood there dumbfounded. "How fast?" I asked, finally.

"Not sure. All that was reported was that he made it in under 24 hours."

I sighed. It was over. Dean had done the coveted linkup, and he'd done it in less than 24 hours. He was officially *the first*. I remember feeling heartbroken. Unlike the other guys on the Yosemite climbing scene— who were too cool to care (or pretended like they were too cool to care) whose name was on which record—I actually did care. I wasn't a champion sport climber or a world-class free climber or a daring free soloist, but I could climb big hunks of granite really fast. It had become my thing.

"You want to go get a sandwich?" Shipoopi asked, giving me a pat on the back.

I thought about it, but only for a second. I had been visualizing doing the two giant routes in my mind for months, and the idea had become an unstoppable force that I needed to go through with. I was committed, both to myself and to my "accountability partners."

"Nah," I said. "I want to finish what I started. I'm going to rope-solo the Nose—it's not like I have anything else planned this afternoon."

"All right, buddy. I'll see you later," Shipoopi said.

Walking the rest of the way to the base of the Nose, I had an interesting realization. I didn't fault Dean for doing what he did. I can't say I would have jumped on a plane to grab the first El Cap–Half Dome linkup title, but I understood how important of a milestone it was to be first on. I was 35 years old, which wasn't *that* far from the 25-year-old version of myself who'd left his job at Parker Seals and moved into his van to chase big dreams in Yosemite.

As I walked through the woods, I thought back to the younger version of myself in the early 1990s. For the first time, I wondered what guys like Peter Croft and Steve Gerberding—the veterans of the time—must have thought of me: Hollywood Hans, bursting onto the scene and aggressively going after any and all records on the Nose. In that respect, Dean and I were a hell of a lot alike.

When I reached the base of El Capitan, all extraneous thoughts left my mind: It was time to climb. I still held the roped-solo speed record on the Nose, a time of 14:11, that I'd set in 1993. I was determined to best it. I used the standard roped-solo technique: Climb the pitch as fast as possible, rap back down, and then clean the pitch as I jugged back up. But I also employed a new method on the easiest pitches, like the ones between Do It Tower and El Cap Tower. Instead of using a rope, I free-soloed, keeping a #3 cam clipped into a daisy chain at the ready for the times when I got sketched out and needed to stick a piece of gear into the wall for peace of mind. The new method shaved 31 minutes off my 1993 record, for a time of 13:40.

In the end I got the linkup in under 24 hours—20:39 to be exact. It was a great accomplishment, no doubt, but I still felt disappointed not to have gotten the milestone first. In bummer situations like that, I've made it a practice to look for the positive. I noted on Speedclimb.com that I was the first person ever to link up Half Dome and El Cap, in that order, in a day (Dean had done it in the reverse). I decided to focus on feeling good about that.

My girlfriend didn't want to climb the Nose with me—an enigma we were debating on a Friday night in November. She'd driven to Yosemite for a visit and announced that she was ready to go up El Capitan. I assumed we'd climb the Nose. She had other ideas.

"Climbing the Nose with you would be like cheating," Jacki said.

"Don't think of it as cheating, think of it as being mentored," I said.

"You've climbed it like thirty times. You have the whole thing memorized," she said. "Where's the adventure in that for me?"

"Thirty-two times," I corrected her.

"I was thinking we could do the Salathé," she said.

"The Salathé is right next to the Nose," I argued. "Why not just do the Nose?"

"I will do the Nose," Jacki said firmly. "Just not with you."

I had one more card to play. I knew Jacki appreciated history. "But the Nose is the original line up El Capitan," I said. "It's tradition to do it first."

"That's a good point," Jacki said, pursing her perfect lips. "But wasn't the Salathé *your* first route on El Cap?"

She had me. I'd climbed the Salathé in 1987, the year before Mike and I made our first attempt on the Nose.

"Fine," I said. "We'll do the Salathé. But I want to climb the Nose with you. Someday."

"Okay, dear," she said, and went into the bathroom to brush her teeth.

The following year, in 2000, a young sport climber named Beth Rodden started asking me about the Nose. I knew Beth and her parents from the climbing-competition scene in the Bay Area. Beth was a climbing prodigy, winning her first Junior National Championship in 1996 at age 16. She successfully defended her title in 1997 and 1998 and also started competing at the adult level. In 1998 she took third in the women's division at the American Sport Climbing Federation Fall Nationals as an 85-pound 18-year-old. That same year she climbed To Bolt or Not to Be at Smith Rock in Oregon, becoming the youngest woman to ascend 5.14a.

In 1999 Lynn Hill invited Beth to join her, along with Nancy Feagin and Kath Pyke, on the first all-female ascent of the massive granite domes of Madagascar's Tsaranoro Massif. Beth's experience in "Africa's Yosemite" was her first significant multipitch trad climb. And now she wanted to climb the Nose.

"It's still too cold," I told Beth in March when she asked me about it again at the climbing gym. "Let's wait a couple weeks until it warms up."

"No way, I want to do it now," she said. "Besides, how cold can it be?" Spoken with the naivety of a California girl. Still, I appreciated her gumption.

"All right," I said. "Next weekend."

I counted on Jacki's maternal instinct kicking in when I told her on the phone that I'd agreed to take Beth Rodden up the Nose.

"But she's just a kid," Jacki said.

"Not anymore," I said. "She's 20."

"Does she have enough experience?" Jacki asked.

"She did Tsaranoro with Lynn Hill," I said. "That had to be at least fifteen pitches."

"Still," Jacki said. "You should have someone else up there. One person can lead and one person can stay on the back end of the rope coaching Beth."

I kept quiet. I knew Jacki would be the perfect person for the job. And once she had a moment to think it through, I hoped she'd offer. I waited. She didn't budge. I threw my last bit of bait:

"I could probably convince Shipoopi."

Jacki groaned. "Having to deal with the two of you and your antics for three days straight could be enough to scare Beth off big-wall climbing forever."

Bait swallowed. I reeled her in. "Well, I don't know anyone else I'd trust to do this right. Except you."

Jacki sighed. "Oh all right," she conceded. "I'll do it. I was planning on coming to visit this weekend anyway."

And so I got Jacki to climb the Nose with me.

Jacki, Beth, and I set out for the base of the Nose at 4:30 a.m., following a routine that had become so familiar that I could do it in my sleep. I planned for us to make it to El Cap Tower (base of pitch 15) for the first night, and Camp VI (top of pitch 26) for the second. We'd stuffed down jackets and hats into the haul bag, anticipating frigid temperatures at night. I brought three ropes—one for the leader and follower, one for the third person to jug up, and one for the pig.

I led the first few pitches, and Jacki and Beth took turns belaying. They also switched off who would follow and remove my pro and who would jug up the second rope. Jacki took over the lead for Stove Legs, and I found Beth to be completely competent at the back end of the rope— whether following or jugging. As we got closer to the end of the day, I decided to give her a shot at leading pitch 13, the 5.9 off of Dolt Tower.

Beth's eyes widened when I told her it was her turn to lead. "Have you seen me lead trad?" she said.

"Everyone has to start somewhere," I replied.

Jacki handed over the 10-pound rack to Beth. The cams hung below her knees. We made sure she was tied into the lead line and had both the second rope and the pig's rope clipped to her harness. Just feeling the weight of all that gear was a first for her.

Beth glanced up at the off-width chimney.

"Don't get too deep into the crack," I told her. "Look for features to use outside it."

Beth nodded and stepped up onto the wall. Jacki snapped photos with my new digital camera, a 1.3-megapixel Olympus. Beth managed to look fierce for the camera, or maybe she was just plain pissed at us for making her lead, it was hard to tell. But whatever her mental state, Beth pulled off the physical execution, free-climbing a 100-foot-long pitch some 1,500 feet above the ground. When she reached the bolts, she set up an equalized anchor, just as Lynn Hill had taught her in Madagascar, and clipped in.

"Nice work on the big stone," I called up. Beth looked down and smiled. "Off belay," she said.

Before I could start to follow, I heard a thud from above.

"Beth!" Jacki called up, fear in her eyes.

"I'm okay," she said in a muffled voice. Then her red face appeared. "I tried to haul."

Jacki giggled. "Well, the haul bag didn't move," she said.

"Wait for me to get up there," I called up. "That bag weighs more than you do."

When I reached the top of the pitch, Beth looked embarrassed. "I watched Lynn Hill haul plenty of times on Tsaranoro, and she's no bigger than me," she said.

"One thing at a time, Grasshopper."

Sleeping on El Cap Tower was rough. The temperature had plunged, and our clothes felt cold and clammy from the light sweat we'd worked up during the day. We donned our insulated jackets, and Beth even slept with her helmet on. Still, I'm pretty sure she froze. I know I did, and I slept poorly because of it.

The next day Beth was content to follow and jug. She didn't ask to try leading again. When we reached the Great Roof at pitch 22, I told her I'd taken Lynn Hill up the Nose on a reconnaissance climb before she freed it in 1993. "The Great Roof was one of her biggest challenges," I told Beth. "The ridiculously thin crack leading up to the roof gets even worse when it turns beneath it. And there's pretty much nothing for your feet."

Beth looked up. "Wow," she said. "What's it rated?"

"5.13b," I said. "You've climbed harder."

I didn't want to push Beth too far outside of her comfort zone, but she was one of the few people I'd encountered who had a legitimate shot at someday repeating Lynn's free ascent of the Nose.

"Want to try?" I asked.

Beth hesitated.

"It's fun," I said with a grin.

Beth snorted. "Fun? The 5.9s on this route are harder than To Bolt," she said, referring to the 5.14a she'd climbed. "I'd hate to see what a 13b on the Nose feels like."

But Beth gave it a try all the same.

As Jacki belayed, I watched Beth lieback the finger crack that started the pitch, using her hands and feet in opposition to inch her way upward. About 20 feet up I heard her breathing start to come out in heaves. She had the technique but not the endurance. It didn't help that there was some water, spring runoff, still seeping from the crack. Beth made it a third of the way to the roof, about the length of the wall in the climbing gym, before bailing.

I felt proud of her and told her so, but she was bummed. "There's no way I'm ever going to free-climb the Nose," she said.

"The first time Lynn Hill climbed the Nose in 1979, she didn't free-climb it. It was all aid climbing back then," I told her. "Give yourself a chance."

That night was just as chilly as the first, and come morning the sky was gray and gloomy. "Looks like the potential for a storm," Jacki said, breaking out the bagels and cream cheese.

I knew that on El Capitan, storms roll in from the north, and any visibility in that direction is blocked by the wall itself. It could be sunny over there, or dark storm clouds could be headed our way. I didn't want to risk freezing rain and lightning—not with California's top sport climber on my watch anyway, and certainly not with the love of my life.

"I want to get us off the rock as soon as possible," I told Jacki and Beth. "New plan: I'll lead all the pitches, Jacki will follow, and Beth will jug the second rope."

We hurried through breakfast and got moving. With only six pitches to go, and our new plan in effect, we topped out in 3 hours. Standing on El Capitan, we could finally see the other side of the sky and realized we weren't in danger of getting rained out. So we took a moment to high-five, hug, and enjoy the view. "I can't believe I did it," Beth kept saying over and over.

On the hike down she told us that on Tsaranoro she didn't get to top out—she had a sponsor commitment that required her to leave a week earlier than the rest of the team. Standing on top of El Capitan had been a huge moment for her. But she'd paid a price—she was utterly exhausted and could barely lift her feet to walk. I told her the fatigue was a normal part of a first big-wall ascent. Her response: "I think I'm going to stick to bouldering for a while."

"A while" turned out to be two months. In May Beth and Tommy Caldwell nabbed the first free ascent (FFA) of Lurking Fear, a nineteen-pitch, 2,000-foot climb to the far left of the Nose. The feat put both Beth and Tommy on the map as big-wall free climbers. At that time, only three of the sixty or so routes on El Cap had gone free. One of Beth's biggest moment came in 2005 when she and Tommy repeated Lynn Hill's free climb of the Nose.

Jacki and I got married on October 7, 2000, in El Cap Meadow, against the backdrop of the Nose, the proudest line in Yosemite. It was a mild Indian summer day, complete with an azure sky and billowy white clouds. Jacki wore a simple pale-blue dress with cap sleeves and carried a bouquet of bay laurel and calla lilies. My mom was there, along with my two brothers and a handful of friends. Shipoopi, who'd gotten deputized by the county of Mariposa, performed the wedding, along with Jacqueline Gardner, one of Jacki's best friends.

Later that month Jacki and I closed on a condo in the Bay Area that she'd purchased with money from her modeling earnings. It was exactly 3 hours and 10 minutes, including a bathroom break, from El Cap Meadow. Our first child, Marianna, was born the day after Thanksgiving. Suddenly, I had two homes, a wife, and a kid. I needed a different way to earn money than traveling around competing in sport-climbing competitions—something more like a real job.

I took a part-time position with Touchstone Climbing, a local company that had opened its first climbing gym in 1995 in San Francisco. Touchstone had since opened four more climbing gyms, most recently in Sacramento, and needed some marketing help. As part of my new job, I made the 75-minute drive from the condo in Lafayette to Sacramento twice a week.

The job didn't seem to negatively impact my climbing. That first summer, in 2001, I set more records in Yosemite than ever before: In June Jacki and I made the fastest male-female ascent of Lurking Fear (14:18). In July I made the first one-day ascent (FOD) of Flight of the Albatross—a twenty-one-pitch, 2,900-foot route on El Cap, two routes left of the Nose—with Kelly Simard and Brian McCray (14:50). Shipoopi, his wife Heather Baer, and I got the FOD of New Jersey Turnpike on the southeast face (16:09), and then Shipoopi, Jacki, and I set the speed record on Mr. Midwest (7:40), located on the far left side of El Capitan near the West Face.

For the Nose, I had a fun new project planned for September. Beth Rodden and I teamed up to guide the youngest climbers ever up the route: Scott Cory, age 11, and Tori Allen, age 13. Both were already climbing superstars. At age 7, Scott on-sighted (made a clean ascent with no falls or beta) Yaak Crack, a 5.11d sport-climb in Nevada. At age 8, he became the youngest member ever of the United States Youth Climbing Team. By age 10, he'd on-sighted his first 5.13—Voodoo Doll in Thailand. I knew Scott and his family well from the local climbing gym. Tori Allen started climbing when she was 10, won her first Junior National Championship when she was 11, and was a professional climber with big-name sponsors, including Nike, Red Bull, and Oakley, by the time she was 12. She remains the only climber I know of that had an action figure made in her likeness.

These kids were part of the X Games generation, and in true Hollywood Hans style, I envisioned their first ascent of the Nose as a movie. Steve Edwards, an old college buddy of mine who dabbled in film production, and I were still in touch and occasionally climbed together. Back then, film was going from analog to digital, and we enjoyed geeking out on the latest technology. Every time Steve and I hung out, we'd talk about doing some sort of climbing film together. I just hadn't found a subject I felt strongly enough about—until now.

I recruited Shipoopi and Tommy Caldwell as riggers and adventure filmmaker Rob Raker as the director of photography. Edwards later sought out another college friend, Alan Bell, an award-winning film editor who would go on to work on dozens of big films including *The Hunger Games*, to do the editing.

We spent four days on the wall, between climbing and filming. It was the first time I had to tell someone (Tori) not to bring makeup on an ascent. She snuck it into her backpack anyway and pulled out her mascara on Dolt Tower to reapply. Scott, two years her junior, adopted the "bratty little brother" role, cajoling her any chance he got. It was hard to say who was more hilarious, the tweens, whom we dubbed "the Wall Rats," or Shipoopi, who was basically an overgrown child: the Rat King. It was quite possibly the most fun anyone's ever had on a big wall. I loved the lighthearted silliness and looked forward to my daughter, Marianna, being old enough to climb.

Two days after the Wall Rats and crew topped out on El Capitan, the 9/11 attacks occurred. Scott Cory lifted everyone's spirits when he began training to become the youngest person to climb the Nose in a day, as a fund-raiser for the spouses and children of the New York City firefighters, police officers, and uniformed Port Authority personnel who'd lost their lives. He returned October 2 and, accompanied by Beth and Tommy, sent the Nose in 13 hours, raising nearly $10,000.

Wall Rats took considerably longer to come together—five years— mostly because Steve and Alan were volunteering their time to work on it. But it was worth the wait. *Wall Rats* premiered January 16, 2006, at the Wild and Scenic Environmental Film Festival in Nevada City, California, where it won Best Children's Film. The 59-minute film went on to screen at several notable film festivals in the West that year, including Boulder Adventure Film, winning Best Kids' Film, and Telluride Mountainfilm Festival, winning the Audience Choice Award.

I already knew Tommy Caldwell from the competition circuit, and after the *Wall Rats* ascent, we decided to climb the Nose, just the two of us. We weren't going after my and Peter Croft's speed record, but we were definitely planning to climb it fast. Tommy is a strong, tenacious free climber who would go on to free-climb all the most notable big walls in Yosemite, culminating in January 2015 with the Dawn Wall on El Capitan (located just to the right of the Nose), believed to be the hardest free climb in the world.

When I met Tommy in El Cap Meadow on a mild September morning for the climb, I felt awful—dead-tired and achy. And not in the got-woken-up-by-a-hungry-baby kind of tired. More like the coming-down-with-a-nasty-virus kind of tired. "I'm not feeling so great," I told Tommy.

"So we're only going to climb the Nose in like 6 hours?" he joked.

"I don't feel *that* bad," I said. "Five, tops."

I wasn't joking. There are only six pitches on the Nose that are rated 5.12 or harder, and not every move on the pitch is of that caliber (a pitch is rated according to its most challenging move). With Tommy's free-climbing skills, I knew we'd be able to free-climb—which is way faster than aid climbing—about 2,500 of the 3,000 feet.

We led in blocks, and I took the first four pitches to Sickle Ledge. I noticed I felt a bit better once we were on the wall. Tommy took over and got us through Stove Legs, and then we motored through the easy pitches between Dolt Tower and El Cap Tower by simul-climbing. I led us through the flakes, the King Swing, and the Grey Bands before I started to feel sick again. We'd been at it for 2 hours and 31 minutes.

I forced myself to eat an energy bar while Tommy led off Camp IV and then worked his magic on the Great Roof.

When it was my turn to take over the lead at Camp V, I still didn't feel any better. I considered telling Tommy that I felt too sick to lead, but I hoped that once I got moving I'd feel better the way I had at the start. It turned out to be wishful thinking. Pitch 25 has been a notoriously tough one for me—the one where I'd turned the lead back over to Mike Lopez on my first ascent. About halfway up I felt carsick, like I was going to throw up. I conceded that it just wasn't my day and lowered back down to the start of the pitch.

"I didn't want to puke on you," I told Tommy. "Think you can finish this?"

Without any hesitation, Tommy took over the rest of the climb, leading the last seven pitches to the top. I checked the watch when I topped out. We'd climbed the Nose in 4:31, only 9 minutes shy of the record I held with Peter Croft. I may have been running a fever, but my mind was able to process what an incredible speed climber Tommy was, and I told him so.

"Don't get any ideas, Hans," he said with a smile.

"But . . ."

"Free climbing is my thing," he said. "That's where I need to put all my energy."

I couldn't help but respect that. I felt the same way about climbing fast.

Meanwhile, Dean Potter and Timmy O'Neill partnered to attempt the most ambitious linkup to date: an enchainment of Half Dome, Mount Watkins, and El Capitan (following the Nose route, of course) in 24 hours or less. They pulled it off in 23:35. I remember thinking about the first big-wall climbers in Yosemite in the 1950s and imagining how the idea of linking three Grade VI walls on three different cliffs in one day would have blown their minds.

I'd heard that Dean and Timmy also had their eye on the speed record on the Nose—mine and Peter's was the last long-standing speed record left in the valley. They went for it in October, not only breaking the record but breaking the 4-hour barrier: They posted a time of 3:59:35. From that point forward, the Nose speed record would always be measured in seconds.

I was fairly certain that Shipoopi and I could do it faster. Dean and Timmy had only cut 23 minutes off a time that Peter and I had set nine years prior. The climbing techniques alone had evolved to be so much more efficient than they were back then. Heck, I'd almost set a new record with the flu. But Shipoopi wasn't interested. "Nah, man, that time is already really fast," he said. "There's other fish to fry."

It took me a moment, but then I understood what he was saying. There were still routes on El Capitan that had never been climbed in less than a day. And others where the "record" time was still double-digit hours. What was the point in whittling a few seconds, or minutes, off the speed record on the Nose, when other routes still needed to be honed by hours, if not days?

Part of me agreed with Shipoopi, but a bigger part of me didn't. It was the Nose, after all, the proudest, most sought-after line in Yosemite. If any speed record should be measured down to the second, this was the one. It dawned on me that I would rather hold one speed record on the Nose than ten speed records on lesser routes.

With my newfound realization and Shipoopi's blessing, I put a call out to my other climbing friends. I had one, maybe two, weeks left to find someone to go up there and retake the record before the winter weather moved in. I could have waited for next season, but having a new baby had taught me that life wasn't so predictable anymore. I couldn't count on being able to spend the same amount of time in Yosemite next season or being able to achieve the same level of fitness.

I sent out a couple e-mails and got a response from my good friend Jim Herson. Like me, he was a new dad in the Bay Area, worked an "ordinary" job, and loved climbing fast. (He was the one I'd set the speed record of 1:53 with on the Regular Northwest Face of Half Dome in 1999).

The only problem was that Jim's current fixation was the Salathé, the Nose's next-door neighbor. He was in the midst of a project to free-climb it. "I'm not driving out to Yosemite just for the Nose," he told me on the phone.

"Okay," I said. "Think of it as the approach to the Salathé."

"Go on," he said.

"We'll speed-climb the Nose in the morning, then walk over to the top of the Salathé and set up a toprope so you can work on free climbing the Salathé Headwall. I'll belay you as long as you want."

"Sold," said Jim.

We met in El Cap Meadow on Sunday morning, October 28, 2001, to sort gear. The autumn sun had just risen. I had a new plan for leading in blocks: We'd cut the route in half, each taking one huge block. We started climbing at 9:33 a.m. with Jim on lead, and flew through the first four pitches to reach Sickle Ledge in 21 minutes. Normally, I would switch out the lead there, but with the new protocol, I placed the pieces of gear I'd cleaned while following Jim back onto his rack and he continued leading, taking us up to Boot Flake at pitch 16.

I took over the lead there, and made sure to note what time Jim hit Camp IV, the approximate halfway point. "We're at 1:59," I called down. "On track!" We were on track to go sub–4 hours, so long as we could keep the same pace, or better yet, speed up a bit. I focused on moving as fast as

I could. Then, as I was leading the Great Roof (pitch 22), I happened to glance down at Jim and noticed he'd taken off his shoe. *What on earth?* I thought.

Jim was still fiddling with his shoe when I anchored into the bolts at the end of the Great Roof pitch. "What's going on?" I yelled down, trying to keep my voice from rising to a frenzied crescendo.

"Shoelace broke," Jim called back cheerily. He was relishing the first real break he'd had since we'd started.

I hung there in my harness, waiting, as precious minutes ticked away. Jim yanked the ratty, frayed string out of his chalk bag and fed it through the eyelets of his climbing shoe. "Way to go, MacGyver," I called down, referring to the old action-adventure television series. Finally, he started up the crack leading to the Great Roof.

Go time. My heart was pounding. I needed to climb the nine pitches still between us and the top faster than I ever had in order to make up for the lost time. At Camp VI (pitch 26), the stopwatch said 3:24. Could I make it to the top in a half hour? Maybe. Jim and I didn't speak; I was in what he called my "catatonic state" as I threw myself up the wall.

Jim hung with me, getting much more than a warm-up for the Salathé. Final time: 3:57:27. We'd climbed the Nose 2 minutes and 7 seconds faster than Dean and Timmy.

A couple days later, I was getting in one final climb of the season with my buddy Dan Dunkle on the Aquarian Wall, a twenty-pitch, 2,000-foot route on El Capitan just right of Lurking Fear, when I heard a commotion in El Cap Meadow. Crowds only gathered for one route, the Nose. And the level of noise made it pretty clear what had just happened.

"Dean and Timmy just took back the speed record on the Nose," I told Dan.

"Wow," he said. "This is getting crazy."

It kind of was. I'd never known a Yosemite speed record to change hands four times in just a couple weeks. The Nose had taken the game of one-upmanship to a new level.

Dan and I were in the midst of a three-day ascent, and the following day I took a bad fall.

As I peeled off the wall, my right hand grazed a small vertical edge, and reflexively clamped down. Pain shot through my fingertips as the full force of the fall yanked me down to the last piece of pro I'd placed. I hung in my harness for a moment to catch my breath.

"You okay?" Dan asked.

"I think so," I said, and resumed climbing. But as soon as I tried to grab on with my left hand, I experienced a jolt of searing pain so intense that I yelped. The middle and ring fingers were no longer working. Not without blinding pain anyway. I wrapped a sling around my wrist with a carabiner at one end and used it as a claw to finish the pitch.

That night on the wall, I slept terribly. As long as I didn't move my hand, the pain was a tolerable dull ache. But even the smallest shift sent sharp shock waves through my fingertips, akin to being stabbed with an ice pick. By the time we'd topped out and hiked 4 hours back to the valley floor, I couldn't use my left hand at all.

We got the official news about Dean and Timmy as soon as we got down. Their time was 3:24:20—more than 30 minutes faster than mine and Jim's. With my hand feeling the way it did, I knew my season was over. I most likely had some serious rehab ahead of me. And some thinking to do: How hard was I willing to fight for the speed record on the Nose?

CHAPTER 8

The Need for Speed

"No climbing," said Jacki, raising her eyes from the book she was reading as I tried to sneak out of the house with my climbing shoes.

"It's not climbing, it's, um, physical therapy."

We'd been having different flavors of the same argument for a couple days now. I'd suffered two broken fingers from my fall on the Aquarian Wall, which meant no climbing for four to six weeks. But the way I saw it, the recovery guideline was overly conservative. I'd torn the tendons that wrap around my fingertips hard enough that they'd pulled tiny specks of bone off with them. My bones weren't fractured; more like frayed. It logically followed that my climbing downtime should be shorter than four to six weeks—say, half that time. It had been about three weeks already. I took another step toward the front door.

"All you have to do is follow the doctor's orders," Jacki said. "It's not that hard."

What she didn't know was that I hadn't actually gone to the doctor. They're expensive and I never like what they have to say about the amount of time I need to take off from my favorite activity. I'd long ago learned to self-diagnose, or in this particular case, go to the dentist.

One of my climbing buddies had a dental practice in East Bay. He'd x-rayed my fingertips using that little cylinder they press against your cheek to x-ray your teeth. He pointed out the detached flecks of bone floating around two of my fingers. "Those are technically considered a break," he explained. "But there's really not much you can do about it except wait for it to heal."

I'd gone home and used the Internet to research recovery time for broken fingers. That's where I'd gotten the four to six weeks. Then I confirmed the information with my brother-in-law, an orthopedic surgeon. Rather than confess all this to Jacki, I put my climbing shoes down and slunk back into the living room. I could wait another week to start climbing again. Maybe.

With the forced time off from the gym, I had some free time to reevaluate my climbing career. I didn't miss competing in sport climbing. I was happy to let the new generation of younger, stronger free climbers like Chris Sharma crush it in the X Games and beyond. I got my fix by helping to run local climbing comps in the Bay Area.

In Yosemite the scene was also shifting. The climbers I'd looked up to for more than a decade were not only losing their hair but also their ability to push the limits on big walls. My own climbing partners were in their late 30s/early 40s with serious jobs, serious relationships, and serious responsibilities. And behind them, chomping at the bit, was the new crop of big-wall climbers: the Tommy Caldwells and Dean Potters.

I wasn't sure where I fit in Yosemite. I wasn't part of the free-climbing, free-soloing, hard-partying faction. Nor was I interested in first ascents of new lines up El Capitan or ascending hard aid-climbing routes, like the generation before me seemed to so thoroughly enjoy. What I liked was climbing light and fast. The faster, the better, in fact. I didn't subscribe to Shipoopi's notion that there was such a thing as *too fast*.

Or did I? Dean's assault on the speed record on the Nose last season had left me feeling a bit gun-shy. It didn't help that *Sports Illustrated*

interviewed me for a feature story that they titled "The El Capitan Climbing War." The writer described me as Dean's "longtime rival" and wrote
that Dean was "barely able to conceal his contempt" when I gave him and
Timmy a pint of Ben & Jerry's chocolate fudge ice cream as a congratula-
tion. Were Dean and I at war? I hadn't thought so. But suddenly I wasn't
sure. About anything.

By March I was back to regular training at the rock gym. My bro-
ken fingers weren't quite at full strength, but they would come around.
I hoped. Jacki and I took our first weekend trip of the new season to
Yosemite. We brought Marianna, who was just starting to walk. Jacki and
I talked, as we so often did on the 3-hour drive to our place in Yosemite
West, about our hopes and dreams and plans for the future.

"Before I get pregnant again, I want to try to become the first woman
to rope-solo the Nose," she said.

I loved the idea—both of having another baby with Jacki and of her
going after a huge goal on the Nose.

The next weekend, Jacki and I did a warm-up run on the Nose with
a friend of ours from the climbing gym, Harry Pali, who was turning 50
and wanted to do something monumental for the occasion. What's more
monumental than climbing the Nose? We spent two days on the ascent.
I got the chance to test out my fingers, at a gentleman's pace, on a big
wall. Jacki got to do some reconnaissance for her roped-solo attempt, and
Harry got his birthday bragging rights.

Jacki set June 13, 2002, as the date for her attempt. I rallied Bay Area
climbing friend and photographer Jim Thornburg to help me chronicle
her climb on film and video. Jacki declined. "I don't want my husband on
the wall with me," she said. "I need to do this on my own."

"You will be," I said. "I'll be guiding the photographer and shooting
the second camera."

She still hesitated.

"Don't make me send Shipoopi," I said.

I knew that Jacki knew that there was no one better equipped than me to assist Jim Thornburg in filming and photographing her on the Nose. Besides having the route memorized, I'd gotten professional film crew experience during *Wall Rats*, and even had a chance to hone those skills by filming my friend Bill Wright's NIAD ascent earlier in the season.

"Besides, would it be so bad to have your husband around?" I said. "We could cuddle on El Cap Tower."

"It has to stay strictly professional," she said. "You're not allowed to act like my husband."

"Fine," I said.

"Or think like my husband."

"I'll do my best," I said.

On the day of Jacki's attempt, at sunrise, Marianna and I walked her to the approach. I wasn't in professional photographer mode yet—Jim and I would meet Jacki at Dolt Tower on her second day—so I was "allowed" to give her a kiss before she started up the wall. I held Marianna and we waved goodbye to Mamma. Jacki planned to spend five days and four nights on the Nose—the longest she'd ever been away from our baby.

I tracked her progress from El Cap Meadow using binoculars. I pointed out the approximate spot on the wall to Marianna. "Mamma's up there." On the second day Jim and I headed up to get some action shots of Jacki. We spent the night on the same ledge as her but as far on the other side as possible. It was more challenging than I thought for me not to "invade" her solo experience. I wanted so badly to share it with her. But I kept my promise and kept my distance.

For Jacki's last night on the Nose, Jim and I camped at the top of El Capitan so we could film her finishing the next morning. I'm pretty sure that watching Jacki Adams Florine crest the lip of the headwall and scramble up the slab to the top of the Nose is the most beautiful thing I've ever witnessed. It took everything for me to just stand by idly as she painstakingly hauled up her gear and carefully coiled her rope. Jacki noticed I was hovering and gave me a tired smile. "No beta," she said.

Since then, only one other woman has rope-soled the Nose: Climbing guide Jes Meiris in 2014. Jes chose to do it in a single push instead of a multiday expedition. Jacki, as I'd already learned, preferred the journey.

By then my fingers were feeling strong enough to start climbing fast for long stretches at a time. Jacki and I did a 13-hour ascent of the Regular Northwest Face of Half Dome, another one of her "to-dos" before getting pregnant. In July I took a 10.5-hour run up the Nose with my friend Mark Gain. Afterward, standing on top of El Capitan and staring down at the crescent-shaped meadow set among the broccoli-size forest, one thing was clear: I could do it faster. Way faster.

Whatever bullshit the media was throwing down about me and Dean suddenly seemed irrelevant. I knew in that moment that I would go for the speed record on the Nose again. The key would be finding a willing and able partner to try for a sub-3:30 ascent. Coincidentally, I returned home to find an e-mail from one of the fastest free climbers on earth waiting in my inbox.

I'd first met Yuji Hirayama in the early 1990s on the World Cup circuit. Back then, he was barely out of his teenage years. He would go on, in 1998, to become the first Asian to win a World Cup competition. We'd become friends the year prior, in 1997, when he came to Yosemite to try free climbing the Salathé. At that point in time, only three others had successfully freed it. Yuji was hoping to on-sight it, to make a clean ascent with no prior practice or beta, which I'd thought was admirably ambitious.

In 1997 I'd spent two days on the Salathé with Yuji and his climbing partner, helping with the hauling, belaying, and logistics. Yuji didn't get the on-sight due to taking a couple falls on the notoriously tricky headwall at the top, but he did nab the fourth free ascent of the Salathé. In "celebration," I'd taken him up the Nose, spending two days and one night on wall. Yuji, of course, wanted to free-climb as much of the Nose as possible. With the exception of 15 feet on the Great Roof and 10 feet on the Changing Corners pitch, we did exactly that.

I opened Yuji's e-mail. He wrote that he was returning to Yosemite in September to finish the job on the Salathé. "I want to climb it clean, no falls this time," he wrote. "And I want to do it in a day."

I was in, with one condition: "Can we climb the Nose fast while we're at it?" I wrote.

"I don't see why not," was his reply.

I'd found my willing and able partner.

But first, I had another important climb to tackle. I'd recently hit my ninety-ninth ascent of El Capitan and wanted to do something significant to mark my one hundredth. I knew of only one other climber who had made ninety-nine ascents of El Cap: Steve Gerberding. I'd run into him in the valley not too long ago, after making my ninety-eighth ascent. He'd told me to call him when I was ready for one hundred and we'd do it together.

A decade ago Steve had been one of my idols—part of the "climb 'til you drop club" that was setting new records on all the big walls in Yosemite in the late '80s and early '90s by using the "single push" technique. Getting to climb with him was a privilege. I loved the idea that, together, we would become the first people to climb El Cap one hundred times. Looking back, I think the collaboration was extra appealing to me because it flew in the face of the idea of El Capitan as a battleground. I loved competition, but I'd choose collaboration over war any day.

On the phone with Steve, I suggested we choose the Nose for our combined one hundredth ascent. But he had an even better idea: "How about we do a route that neither one of us has ever done before?"

I was game. We settled on the Dihedral Wall, a twenty-six-pitch route located about halfway between the Nose and Lurking Fear. It was first climbed by Ed Cooper, Jim Baldwin, and Glen Denny in 1962, the fourth route established on El Capitan, after the Nose, the Salathé, and Muir Wall.

On September 14, 2002, Steve and I met to sort gear. He was a hardcore aid climber who'd made six first ascents of El Capitan. As such, he was used to bringing four aiders—two for each leg. I, being of the fast and light mentality, said we'd need one, tops. Steve raised an eyebrow but didn't argue. We set out the next morning to climb Dihedral in a day. Like Murphy's Law predicts, I ended up needing that aider and then accidentally dropped it about halfway up the route. I was horrified to tell Steve, but he didn't flinch. Not even an "I told you so." He went to work fashioning a makeshift aider from some discarded rope someone had left on the route.

We sent Dihedral in 14 hours and 6 minutes, setting a new speed record and collectively becoming the first people to climb El Cap one hundred times. Instead of hiking down right away, we spent the night at the top, laying under the stars, trading numbers. Steve was 42 years old and had been climbing El Cap for nineteen years. I was 38 years old and had been climbing El Cap for thirteen years. Of Steve's one hundred ascents on El Cap, he'd done fifty-one different routes. I'd only done twenty-five different routes, because so many of my ascents had been the Nose.

"I guess I'm kind of a one-trick pony," I said.

Steve laughed. "Hans, you can't compare us. You're a racehorse. I'm a mule. I couldn't do what you do any more than you could do what I do."

I closed my eyes, letting the fatigue of the Dihedral Wall climb wash over me. I thought about the first time I'd encountered Steve Gerberding, in 1990. I was making my first speedy ascent of the Nose, with Shipoopi, and we'd passed Steve and Dave Bengston, who were climbing NIAD, around eight pitches in. I remembered how I'd taken an embarrassing whipper on the second pitch and how passing Steve and Dave, two of my heroes, had helped bolster my confidence that I would make it.

I thought back to the speed record on the Nose at that time: 9:30, held by two Europeans. When Shipoopi and I topped out in 8:05, I'd been out-of-my-mind excited. Twelve years later I was aiming to best Dean and Timmy's time of 3:24:20. Yes, Steve Gerberding and I were different animals. We'd each furthered the sport of big-wall climbing in our own way. What a wild ride it had been. I drifted off to sleep with a smile on my lips

Yuji flew in from Tokyo a couple days later. We made an odd couple, his shock of jet black hair to my mane of bleach blond; his short, compact build to my long, lanky one. And he could free-climb at a level I couldn't even dream of. He made quick work of the Salathé in 13 hours, without a single fall. It was the second time, after Tommy Caldwell in 2002, in a time of 19:30, that anyone had free-climbed the Salathé in less than a day.

Watching Yuji gave me an idea for the Nose. What if he led the entire thing? The guy could free-climb for 13 hours straight on the Salathé—surely he could lead 3 hours on the Nose. Timmy and Dean had led in blocks, four to be precise. Not having to switch out leaders would save time. I would stay on the back end, managing the rope, and simul-climbing as much as possible. Timmy and Dean had taken up only twenty cams, an incredibly light rack. With Yuji free-climbing most of the Nose, we could go just as light, if not lighter.

We put my theory into practice on September 23. "It's just a test run," I told Yuji. But the statement was more to calm my own excitement. I felt like a kid at Christmas. I tried to relax and stay smooth. We made it to Sickle Ledge, the first four pitches, in 19 minutes, hitting the midpoint at Camp IV in 1:52, and topping out in 3:27. It wasn't faster than Dean and Timmy's record of 3:24:20, but it was incredibly close for a "test run." Plus, we'd passed seven other parties on the climb, which ate up considerable minutes. Imagine how fast we could go if we had the wall to ourselves and were actually going full throttle?

Yuji wasn't too hard to convince. We agreed to try again on the 29th. Word got out that we had a good shot at breaking the record, and a few dozen people showed up in El Cap Meadow that morning, swelling to about one hundred by the time we finished. My good buddy and future coauthor Bill Wright even flew in from Boulder, Colorado, just to watch.

Yuji stepped onto the wall at 7:15 a.m. We blazed to Sickle Ledge in 16 minutes. At Camp IV my stopwatch read 1:28. We topped out in 2:48:55, breaking both the record time and the 3-hour barrier. Yuji put it best when he told me that the climb felt a lot like running. I thought back to my track-and-field days and dubbed the Nose my vertical marathon.

In the days that followed, I was curious if anyone would take a crack at the record. Timmy O'Neill told *Rock & Ice* magazine that he believed the Nose could go under 2 hours. But as the winter weather moved in, no one tried. It looked like my and Yuji's speed record would hold—at least until spring.

———

I was the new cover model in the family. The January 2003 issue of *Rock & Ice* magazine featured one of Jim Thornburg's photos of me climbing the Nose—tan, shirtless, hair flying, one chalky hand grabbing for a narrow ledge. "Possessed," read the cover line. "Hans Florine's rage against time." Inside was a four-page feature story, including a picture of me in

El Cap Meadow tossing Marianna into the air, straight up the line of the Nose.

"That's hot," Jacki said, her four-month-pregnant baby bump finally starting to show, when she saw the cover. "I like the use of the word 'possessed.' It really personifies the Nose."

"Can I get your autograph?" Shipoopi asked. "I was hoping you could sign my chest."

In the next few years, no one challenged the speed record on the Nose. Dean Potter was likely the most capable (and the most motivated), but after *Climbing* magazine put him on the cover as "Climber of the Year" in December 2002, he seemed content to focus on other interests, including slacklining and BASE jumping. Meanwhile, there continued to be interesting people who wanted to climb the Nose with me—which was all the incentive I needed to make additional ascents.

Between 2003 and 2006 I made it up the Nose another sixteen times. I also worked on a few projects on El Cap's other routes, including partnering with Chris McNamara in 2005 to set a new speed record of 6:27 on the Triple Direct, a fun route that climbs the first ten pitches of the Salathé and then joins up with the Nose.

For my fortieth birthday, I wrote a book with Bill Wright called *Speed Climbing! How to Climb Faster and Better*. It was my way of dealing with aging, I suppose. Sort of like imparting wisdom. I documented the techniques I'd learned over the years including roped-soloing, simul-climbing, safely passing other parties on the wall, equipment, and training. I included a history of speed climbing and a compilation of the speed-climbing records I'd been tracking for more than a decade on Speedclimb.com.

I also put together a CD of audio recordings on how to speed-climb the Nose, pitch by pitch. My son, Pierce, was born in May of 2003, and something about seeing my baby boy for the first time inspired me to leave something behind that he could listen to, in case he lost me the way I had my own father.

El Capitan went back to its rightful role as a beacon of adventure, instead of a battleground. Almost.

In the summer of 2006, Alex and Thomas Huber, two brothers from Germany who were among the top all-around climbers in the world, showed up in Yosemite and announced they were going to break the speed record on the Nose. They brought with them one of the largest film crews ever to descend on Yosemite Valley and a movie budget rumored to be $1 million.

It wouldn't be the first time the Hubers aimed to make history on El Capitan. In 1995 they had scored the second free ascent of the Salathé. In 1998 they nabbed the first free ascent of both El Nino (5.13c, thirty pitches) and Free Rider (5.12d, thirty-seven pitches); in 2000 they made the first free ascent of Golden Gate (5.13, forty pitches); and in 2001, the first free ascent of El Corazon (5.13b, thirty-five pitches). In 2004 they switched from first free ascents to speed, setting the record on the Zodiac (5.7, sixteen pitches) in a blazing 1:51:34. When not in Yosemite, they were making first ascents and setting records on other iconic chunks of granite, like Europe's Mont Blanc and Patagonia's Fitz Roy massif, or climbing 8,000-meter peaks in Nepal like Cho Oyu.

I ran into Thomas and Alex, literally, on the Nose, on June 16. My friend Peter Darmi and I were climbing NIAD and heard the noise from the crowd in El Cap Meadow indicating that the Hubers had stepped onto the rock. I clocked their time to Sickle Ledge and noted that they were on track to break the record. They passed us right before we went into the Stove Legs crack, and I clocked them again just before they disappeared on Dolt Tower. "If they keep it up, they'll break the record by 18 minutes," I told Peter.

"You would know," he said with a grin.

When we topped out, after 14 hours of climbing, the Hubers were gone. But they had a film crew camped up there, and one of the staff gave us the bad news. Thomas had taken a whipper in between the Great Roof and Camp V, crashing into a small ledge and severely bruising his hip and glute before his brother arrested his fall. Needless to say, the Hubers hadn't gotten the record. Thomas was okay to hike down but was in a fair amount of pain and needed to have his hip looked at.

On June 25 I topped out on the Nose again, this time with an old friend of Shipoopi's named Wayne Willoughby, who, despite suffering from the late effects of paralytic polio, and post-polio syndrome, had gone on to become an accomplished climber. Over the course of eight years, Wayne and I had done three other routes on El Cap before taking on the Nose and were feeling pretty darn celebratory at the top—the 22-hour ascent marked the first NIAD by an adaptive climber.

We encountered the Hubers, who were in much lower spirits, up there. Alex told us they'd been relentlessly dissecting the route, training each section, each move, day after day, in order to set a new record time, with a goal of 2:30. They were knackered from the effort, and Alex had a bruise to rival Thomas's from a fall across the meadow at the Cathedral Rocks. He pulled down his pants a bit to reveal a hideous purple hematoma covering his right buttock. "I can barely walk," he said.

"We can show you ten places on the Nose where you can die," Thomas added.

Soon after, the Hubers left Yosemite. Their 95-minute film, *Am Limit* ("To the Limit"), premiered in Germany in March 2007 and told the grisly story of their attempt for the record. While it didn't have a happy ending, the footage they'd captured on-route was unlike anything seen before, putting viewers on the wall with the Hubers, swinging through giant pendulums, stuffing their bloody, taped fingers into thin, jagged cracks, and taking colossal falls while simul-climbing. The *New York Times* called it "daredevil camerawork."

In the fall of 2007, the Huber brothers returned to Yosemite. They hadn't been able to let go of the Nose speed record and were looking for redemption. I was in Italy when they went for the record again. On October 4 I got an e-mail from Alex. "What is the exact time of your Nose record?" he wrote. I sent him back my and Yuji's time: 2:48:55.

"We did it in 2:48:55," he wrote back. "So I guess we have the record, but let us try again. It's not enough." They tried again four days later, whittling the record down to 2:45:45. I admired their ambition but felt disappointed to lose the record. I cajoled myself that losing the speed record on the Nose to Alex and Thomas Huber was an honor. Those guys were the best of the best. And what a hat tip to the Nose that they would put so much effort into it.

In retrospect, it was the perfect opportunity for me to back away gracefully from the race for the Nose. I would be 44 when the Yosemite climbing season resumed the following year, and I'd recently begun full-time employment, working a desk job at the architectural design firm TranSystems to support my young family. But before I had a chance to contemplate that, an e-mail from Yuji appeared in my inbox.

"I know I can do it faster," he wrote, "and you're the only one I trust on the back end of the rope." He wanted to come back in September with a small film crew to air a news segment on prime-time television in Japan. He didn't have to ask Hollywood Hans twice.

My concern was fitness. I hadn't climbed the Nose fast in six years—the last time Yuji was in town. "Can you come in June for some practice climbs first?" I wrote. I knew it was a lot to ask. Yuji had a family of his own. But he agreed. "For you, Hans, yes."

Reclaiming the speed record on the Nose was going to take everything I had. But I felt like this was maybe my last chance, my last push, before I settled into middle age. Luckily, my loving wife gave me her full support. I focused the rest of the year and the following spring on my training. I'd go into Diablo Rock Gym from 4 to 7 a.m., then shower and head to my desk job.

To mimic the effort level required for a 3-hour push on the Nose, I created a workout score sheet—which the staff at Diablo found highly entertaining. I'd get two points for climbing a 5.6, for example, ten points for a 5.9, and fifty points for a 5.12. I figured 1,500 points was equivalent to sending the Nose, so if I climbed thirty different 5.12s in under 3 hours, I'd be done with training for the day. I did the same with exercises: one point for every three push-ups, one point for every five sit-ups, and one point for every pull-up.

"If you can do 1,500 pull-ups in 3 hours, you can probably do the Nose faster than me," I spoke into the camera to Eric Perlman, who was filming a segment on Yuji and my speed attempt on the Nose for his climbing-film series *Stone Masters*.

As soon as the Nose dried out at the end of May, I climbed NIAD three weekends in a row, with three different friends, in preparation for Yuji's arrival. When he got to the valley the last weekend in June, the first thing we did was go for a warm-up on the Nose, in 4:48. The *San Francisco Chronicle* put us on the front page of the paper the next day and then again three days later, when we did our next training session in 3:28. I realized I needed to explain to them that we were "training" before going for the record. Nevertheless, it made me smile that a major newspaper was so engaged in the speed record on the Nose, and that we'd stolen the front page from Barack Obama during the democratic primaries.

Yuji and I used our training sessions to dial in technique—at what points on the wall we needed to be in the same place at the same time so I could hand off the gear I'd cleaned, how Yuji could best navigate the bolt ladders, and where we might short-fix or simul-climb in the upper pitches. On our third training session, on June 29, we pared down the gear to exactly what we needed, and not a single piece more. I made a list:

Eighteen CAMP Nano 24-gram carabiners on BD tiny quickdraws

Five Trango Superfly Lockers

Eleven free biners, BD Nutrinos

Seven long Yates slings with ten biners (two were for slinging the gear and draws)

(ALL the following cams had their own CAMP Nano 24 biner) One gold Camalot, one red, two green, two purple, two orange Metolius Tricams, two yellow, two blue, two purple, one gray.

One cam hook

NO NUTS, that's right NO NUTS (Yosemite cracks are parallel)

One USBA ascender (used for simul-climbing four places)

One set of Petzl ascenders

One set of Yates Speedy Stirrups (prototypes, not available for sale)

One superlight Chris Gonzales's Dynema Etrier

Two harnesses, one Beal, one Petzl

One Yates Big Wall speed rope (made by BlueWater, 9.4 mm cut down to 60 meters)

One Petzl helmet (Hans wore it)

Two chalk bags

Two Highgear watches/altimeters (gain was 2,978 ft.)

One Petzl Grigri (strategically drilled for weight savings, retainer cord attached)

Two wedding rings, not on fingers

Two Double Caffeine Tangerine Powergels

Two 600 ml water bottles

One 10-oz. can Xcyto energy drink

Tech T-shirts and knicker-length pants for each climber

We sent the Nose in 2:47:30, faster than we'd done it when we'd first broken the record together in 2002.

"We're ready," I told Yuji.

We went for the record three days later. Eric Perlman was there filming for *Stone Masters*, as was the local news. Jacki brought the kids; Pierce, our youngest, had just turned 5. Yuji and I moved through the climb like it was a choreographed dance, and in a way, it was. As the follower, the final time came down to me smacking the tree at the top. I hit it at 2:43:33, besting the Hubers by 2 minutes and 12 seconds. The best part was that it was just the dress rehearsal. Yuji was coming back at the end of September with his film crew.

In between, I climbed Carstensz Pyramid—the highest peak in Oceania—with Erik Weihenmayer, the finale of his Seven Summits project. Not exactly the best way to stay in big-wall-climbing shape, but an epic adventure that I couldn't refuse. Then I got sick on the return trip from Indonesia and couldn't climb or train for two weeks. When Yuji returned, I was a wreck over my fitness, or lack thereof. Yuji, with his usual calm demeanor, assured me we were going to ease into it, just like before. We planned three training climbs, followed by a record attempt on October 12. I was still nervous as hell.

We put up a time of 4:07 on our first practice run, getting reacquainted with the moves and techniques. I happily noted that the ascent was 41 minutes faster than our first training climb back in June. Yuji just laughed. "You still got it, Hans," he said.

On October 12 I had more butterflies than usual. I felt that a huge chapter of my life was coming to a close and I wanted to end on a high note. Hell, I wanted to go out with a bang. This was the culmination of everything I'd worked to achieve in rock climbing, the fusion of my sport-climbing comp career with my passion for big-wall climbing, all coming together on my favorite route, which just so happened to be the greatest route on earth.

The biggest crowd ever had gathered in El Cap Meadow—hundreds of people. Besides friends and family, the local news, and Yuji's film crew, NPR was there, as was Tom Frost, a living legend from the golden age of Yosemite climbing, who'd made the second ascent of the Nose, with Royal Robbins, Chuck Pratt, and Joe Fitschen, in 1960. Jacki had a bag full of champagne bottles at the ready to spray us in a victory tunnel—like they did at NASCAR—when we got to the bottom. I usually enjoyed high-pressure situations, felt like they pushed me to do my best, but that morning, for the first time, I felt overwhelmed.

The crisp weather didn't help. I am not built for the cold, or as my wife puts it, "He shakes like a Chihuahua in 50 degrees or less." I'd already donned a long-sleeved fleece and still needed to bum a puffy off a Swedish girl at the base for warm-up.

Yuji and I had a routine by that point. We climbed the first pitch to loosen up and then lowered back down. Before starting the stopwatch, we looked each other dead in the eye, "Safety first, speed second," we said in chorus. It was a promise, from one dad to another, not to do anything stupid. Then we counted down together in Japanese: "*San, ni, ichi!*" I started the timer. It was 10:20 a.m.

In the first four pitches, we passed two parties, which didn't help my nerves as I fretted over losing precious time. I missed an unexpected green cam that Yuji had placed when he stepped over the second team's lead line on pitch 3, and had to backtrack 8 feet to grab it. We hit Sickle Ledge in 18 minutes, slower than the expected 16. Instead of feeling bummed, I drew on my track-and-field experience to remind myself that negative splits are part of setting record-fast times. As my climbing buddy Scott Frye would say: "Start out slow, go, go, go. Start out fast, just won't last."

The first gear handoff went smoothly, as did the pendulums into the Stove Legs, which helped me relax. The cool temperatures were actually beneficial when I was cranking through 400 feet worth of cracks, trying to keep up with Yuji's blistering pace. I hit Dolt Tower in 46 minutes and had to glance at the watch again to make sure I wasn't hallucinating—we were 10 minutes faster than we'd ever gone before.

I got cocky on the King Swing, hamming it up for the camera by doing a little spin move. I missed the grab for the crack and didn't make it to Eagle Ledge, swinging back to the right and having to do it all over (minus the showboating). Yuji didn't seem too upset—we were still 2 minutes ahead of our record time. At Eagle Ledge we gulped our customary Double Caffeine Tangerine Powergel and drank a sports drink—the only place on the route where we refueled.

At Camp IV, the halfway point, I was disappointed to see a time of 1:28—2 minutes slower than our record time. I handed off the gear to Yuji just before he went into the Great Roof and told him where we were at. "I've got this," he said, and then kicked it into another gear. At Camp V, on top of pitch 24, we were tracking at 6 minutes under the record. Yuji was pushing the limits of safety, leading with a huge loop of slack beneath him. A fall could have been catastrophic.

When we reached the shaded dihedrals of the final four pitches, my hands started to feel noticeably cold. I struggled to extract Yuji's pro with numb fingers, cursing the delay. At that point I couldn't waste a single moment to check the stopwatch—all I knew was that I needed to hurry.

When I crested the last lip before the summit, I was gasping for air. I sprinted up the final slab that led to the tree and smacked it, collapsing. I had just enough energy left to stop the watch. It read 2:37:05. We were 6 minutes and 28 seconds faster than our previous record.

Yuji had his prime-time news footage, and I had my grand finale. Timmy O'Neill told a reporter that I was like Gollum in *The Lord of the Rings*; the speed record on the Nose was "My Precious." The comparison made me chuckle. Maybe I'd gotten a little obsessed. But man, what a thrill. In a span of nineteen years, I'd gone from climbing the Nose in 46 hours to just over 2.5. And I'd had the pleasure of watching something that had been my pet project grow into the most coveted speed record in big-wall climbing.

Standing atop El Capitan with Yuji, I felt ready for the next phase of my life—raising a family in the Bay Area with the woman of my dreams, visiting Yosemite on weekends and holidays, and continuing to climb big walls well into my old age, albeit more slowly than before.

The Nose, however, had other plans.

CHAPTER 9

Climb On

July 4, 2009, marked the twentieth anniversary of my first Nose ascent. The day prior, my old college climbing buddy Mike Lopez pulled into the driveway of my Yosemite home. We planned to do Nose in a Day as a commemorative climb. The pace would be slow compared to the speed runs I'd done in the recent past, but still way faster than Mike's and my first time of 46 hours. With NIAD, we'd cut our first time by 70 percent. Not bad for two guys pushing 50.

Although Mike had been living in Joshua Tree for many years, he was more committed to hang gliding than rock climbing, and he was about 20 pounds overweight—a fact he sheepishly admitted as soon as he walked through the front door. "If we're going to climb the Nose in less than a day, I vote you lead," he said.

"Fine by me," I said. "But you're leading the King Swing."

On our first ascent of the Nose, I'd gotten to do the exhilarating pendulum.

"Deal," he said, smiling.

The next morning we reached the base of the Nose at first light, climbing steadily through the morning. I led each pitch, using the combination of free climbing and French free climbing that I'd learned over the years. Mike, despite his forebodings about his fitness level, proved a capable and efficient follower, jugging his way up the rope and cleaning the gear I'd placed with apparent ease.

Moving through the first major features like Sickle Ledge and the Stove Legs, I couldn't help but reflect back on the struggles and doubts that had played out for me and Mike on these lower pitches twenty years earlier. Remembering our misadventure made me realize how much my perspective had shifted; some might say I felt wiser. Through the lens of experience, the giant granite cliff looming over us had morphed from a brutal force of nature to a playground of adventure. The Nose hadn't changed—I had.

We reached the top of Texas Flake right as the sun began its final push to the high point of the sky that indicated noon. From our perch on the narrow flake, we could see El Cap Meadow and the surrounding forest tinged in a soft haze from recent wildfires.

"All right, it's all you," I told Mike as we switched out the lead. "Any last words?"

"It was worth it," Mike said, laughing.

I belayed Mike while he climbed carefully across the bolt ladder that connects Texas and Boot Flakes. I couldn't help but remember how I'd freaked out there during our first Nose climb. I imagined going back in time and telling the 25-year-old Hans that one day he'd be just as comfortable on that exposed bolt ladder as he was hiking to the base. I'm certain the 25-year-old version of myself wouldn't have believed it.

Something I had only recently come to understand was the power of logging years and years of "right practice," specifically about 10,000 hours worth. I'd just read a new book called *Outliers* by Malcolm Gladwell, in which he identifies the "10,000-Hour Rule" as the key to achieving world-class success in any skill, whether sports or music or computer programming. I was perhaps the only person on earth who'd come close to putting in that amount of time on El Capitan.

"You sure this thing's attached?" Mike called out from the bottom of the Boot Flake, breaking my reverie. He was only half joking.

"Nope," I called back, half joking myself. "We expect it's going to peel off the wall any moment."

Mike grunted and then made his way up to the top of the boot, moving as quickly as possible. He wasn't taking any chances. I watched him anchor into the bolts and then I began lowering him down for the King Swing.

"Easy does it," I coached from Texas Flake. "I'm taking you all the way down to the second-to-last bolt on the bolt ladder."

When Mike was in position, sitting in his harness, feet on the wall in front of him, he looked over at me. "Here goes nothing."

I pulled out my camera. Mike jogged across the wall to the right to get some momentum and then left, swinging some 40 feet before grabbing for the small edges on the wall to haul himself over to Eagle Ledge. He wasn't able to keep his purchase and ended up swinging back. "It's harder than it looks," I said. "Think about finessing a sideways crawl into the end of your swing."

Mike steadied himself and then tried again, to the same end. "Try again," I offered. Mike looked up at the anchors, as if to check that they were still holding. Then he took a deep breath, running right and then left, adding in a lateral Spiderman-esque crawl at the end. "That's it!" I yelled.

Mike disappeared behind the corner to Eagle Ledge.

"Yessss!" I heard from across the granite.

Mike and I would top out just after sunset, in 14:11. "No bivy!" he whooped, referring to the fact that we hadn't needed to spend the night on the wall. We hugged it out, and he told me that "next time" he wanted to lead at least a third of the pitches, including the Stove Legs. Mike's since lost 30 pounds. For his fiftieth birthday, he climbed fifty pitches in Joshua Tree. For his sixtieth, in 2018, we plan to climb the Nose again.

Meanwhile, a new rock star was rising in Yosemite. In 2007 a 21-year-old from Sacramento named Alex Honnold free-climbed two classic Yosemite routes, Astroman (5.11c) and Rostrum (5.11c), back-to-back, in a day. And he did it without a rope. Astroman ascends for 1,100 feet, and Rostrum for 800. One mistake—grabbing onto a loose piece of rock or slipping on moisture—would have most likely resulted in a fall and the end of Alex Honnold.

The only other person to have free-soloed Astroman and Rostrum in a day was Peter Croft, in 1987. Since then, no one had tried. Many climbers equated free soloing big walls with a death wish. Derek Hersey, a popular Yosemite climber based in Boulder, Colorado, fell to his death in 1993, at age 39, while free-soloing the Steck-Salathé on Sentinel Rock. Even before the fall, Hersey was known as "Dr. Death" for climbing without a rope.

In 2008 Alex Honnold completed a climb previously considered unthinkable—he free-soloed the 2,000-foot Regular Northwest Face of Half Dome (5.12). He became known in the valley as "that crazy kid who climbs without ropes." But I noticed Alex also did plenty of free climbing *with* ropes, setting several new speed records in the process. Most notably, in 2009, Alex, along with Sean Leary, ratcheted Yuji's free-climbing time of 13 hours on the Salathé down to 8.5 hours.

I'd seen Alex, a gangly guy with a mop of brown hair and a big smile, here and there in the valley, but our paths didn't cross until spring 2010, when I heard he was attempting the speed record on the Nose with Ueli Steck. Steck is a cutting-edge alpinist from Switzerland who is known for going fast and light and blowing the international climbing community's mind with speed ascents in the Alps, like the Eiger North Face in 2:47:33.

I approached Alex the next time I saw him in Yosemite to get the scoop. He told me that Sender Films, the company that cocreated the popular Reel Rock film tour, was on-site getting footage of Ueli Steck for *The Swiss Machine*. They'd asked Alex to take a run up the Nose with Ueli for the camera. Alex said he'd read my book on speed climbing in preparation, and he seemed really excited to try.

While my ego wanted to hold on to the speed record on the Nose for as long as possible, I liked Alex's genuine enthusiasm. It was a good opportunity to try out a new role as mentor. I gave Alex my number if he had any questions or needed advice. He took me up on it, calling a few times during the filming. I enjoyed those talks. Alex has a wry sense of humor and an insatiable curiosity about climbing. I decided that being Yoda was kind of cool.

On Alex and Ueli's first try in May, Ueli was fresh off the plane and still jet-lagged, and he and Alex had never climbed together. Not a great combination for speed. Still, they finished in a more-than-respectable time of 4:40. Then they came back the next day and did it in 4:20. The general sentiment in the valley was that these guys had a legitimate shot at breaking the record. But on a later attempt, Ueli took a horrifying fall, plunging some 80 feet before the rope caught him. The fall ended Ueli's bid for the speed record, and he went back to Europe shortly after.

The experience was enough to get Alex hooked on the Nose. We tried to make plans to climb it together but couldn't get our schedules to jibe. I'd left the architectural-engineering firm to become the manager of Diablo Rock Gym, which had been struggling and needed a new direction. As a result, I was spending the vast majority of my time back in the Bay Area. I'd only climbed the Nose twice in May, and come June, admitted that I wouldn't be back the rest of the season. I needed to commit to my new job.

Still, I watched from afar, which wasn't hard to do with texting, e-mail, and social media (although I'm still waiting for someone to put up a webcam with live feeds of the action on the Nose). In July Alex made a roped-solo attempt on the Nose. Shipoopi had been the first to rope-solo the Nose in less than 24 hours, in 1989. Then I'd set a new record of 14:10 in 1993, which held until 1999 when Dean Potter took it under 13 hours. I'd reclaimed the record in 2006, with a time of 11:41. I had a feeling the torch was about to be passed again. Sure enough, Alex topped out in a blistering 5:50. I was impressed, not only with Alex but with myself—I was able to let the record go with a smile. I looked forward to climbing the Nose with Alex and transferring my years of knowledge to such an astute and competent pupil.

Not long after, Sean Leary, better known as Stanley, decided to see how fast he could climb the Nose. Stanley already owned four other speed-climbing records in Yosemite Valley, in addition to the one he and Alex had set on the Salathé the year prior, and he didn't have too hard of a time convincing his buddy Dean Potter to show him the ropes on the Nose. Stanley and Dean began making speedy practice ascents of the Nose in November.

I was surprised to hear Dean was back after the speed record. He'd undergone a self-proclaimed cleanse from competition, choosing instead to climb as a spiritual pursuit, as an art. He was also heavily involved in aerial pursuits—BASE jumping and wingsuit flying, an endeavor that would take both Stanley's life in 2013 and his own in 2015.

Dean steered clear of me, so I never did find out his reason for rejoining the race for the Nose. He said in the film *Race for the Nose* that he wanted to "leave a mark" before he got too old. He was 38 at the time. Peter Mortimer, the founder of Sender Films, contacted me for an interview for the film. I enjoyed speaking about the speed record for the Nose on camera. It hit me that I'd held the record for the vast majority of the last twenty years. The longest I'd gone without it was eleven months—after

Dean and Timmy took it in 2001. Peter dubbed it "the wildest competition known to man," and I had to agree.

Stanley and Dean cracked my and Yuji's record after five tries. Their new record time of 2:36:45 was only 20 seconds faster than the previous record, but as Dean said for the camera, "The fastest is the fastest, even if it is only 20 seconds."

Race for the Nose was one of Sender Films best works ever, or maybe I'm just biased toward anything that features my favorite rock. The media resurrected the so-called rivalry between me and Dean. Reporters asked me (and still ask me) how I felt about Dean. On a personal level I didn't know Dean at all. On a professional-climbing level, my feeling about Dean, as well as about Stanley, Timmy O'Neill, the Huber brothers, Peter Croft, and anyone who challenged the Nose record, is gratitude for continuing to raise the bar. Without those guys keeping the competition going, I wouldn't have had nearly the same motivation to achieve what I have on the Nose.

Shortly after the film premiered, I saw a call from Alex coming through on my cell. I was pretty sure he was calling under the guise of offering his condolences in order to give me a good ribbing for losing "My Precious." I answered, and braced myself for his dry wit.

"I saw *Race for the Nose*," he said. "Sorry about that."

"Yeah, thanks," I said, somewhat sarcastically.

Alex paused. *Here it comes*, I thought.

"So I was thinking we should take it back," he said. "You know, the record."

I nearly dropped my phone.

"You," I said, "and me, the old guy?"

"Exactly how old are you anyway?"

"Don't worry about it," I said. "Oh, and Alex?"

"What?"

"I'm in."

Alex was well on his way to fame at that point. Sender Films had released *Alone on the Wall*, which chronicled Alex's attempt to free-solo the Regular Northwest Face of Half Dome. The startling photo of Alex standing, without a rope or any protection, on a tiny ledge on Half Dome some 1,800 feet off the valley floor would soon grace the cover of *National Geographic*, and *Outside* magazine would run a feature story on Alex called "No Strings Attached" in the April 2011 issue. Fast-forward a couple more years and Alex Honnold would be rock climbing's closest thing to a household name. Surely, he was capable of setting an unprecedented speed record on the Nose.

But as soon as I hung up the phone, I panicked. I'd made a rash, emotional decision that went against my "transition to Yoda" plan. I felt like a recovering alcoholic about to fall off the wagon. I went home after work and fretted to Jacki about it. She listened for about 2 minutes and then cut me off. "Hans?"

"Yes?" I said.

"Honey, it's not going to hurt anything if you speed-climb the Nose with Alex Honnold. And it will probably be a lot of fun."

I stood very still.

"What about Yuji?" I said.

"Write him a courtesy e-mail," she said. "It's not like you guys made a commitment to be Nose speed-climbing partners 'til death do you part."

She was right. On all counts. I exhaled.

Alex and I met on October 13, 2011, to climb together for the first time—the Nose, of course. He was rock climbing's biggest star and I was the Nose Guru, or at the very least the guy who'd climbed it an unheard-of eighty-three times. Yet on a clear fall day in El Cap Meadow, we were just two guys sorting our gear and debating the rack.

Alex was of a certain mind-set. Let's call it minimal to the point of reckless. I understood his motivation—the less gear on your rack, the lighter and faster you climb. But I had a different perspective: Place enough gear that you feel safe and you will climb faster for it.

"You're bringing a #2?" Alex asked raising his eyebrows. The cam he was referring to is just about the most indispensable piece of gear in climbing the Nose—a device you jam into cracks that are about 2 inches wide, mainly about 100 feet worth of the Stove Legs. I had a flashback to sorting gear with Steve Gerberding for our mutual 100th El Cap ascent, only now I was in the opposite role.

"Actually, I'm bringing two #2s," I said.

Alex's eyes widened. "My hand fits perfectly into a crack that size," he said. "So I'm all set."

Now it was my turn to raise an eyebrow. "This is a test climb, a practice, remember? I'm bringing it."

Alex rolled his eyes. But he didn't let up. "And why are we bringing #3s?"

I sighed. It was the same reason. There's about 120 feet worth of 3-inch-wide cracks in the Stove Legs. And I knew Alex knew that. "Why *wouldn't* we bring #3s?" I asked, looking him square in the eye.

He held my gaze. "What's on the edge of your wrist?"

I wondered if this was some kind of trick question. Before I could muster a smart-aleck answer, he said, "Your hand. It's the same size as a #2 Camalot. Turn your hand to the side and it's the size of a #3. Make a fist and it's a #4. So there you have three pieces of gear that you are already equipped with since birth."

"Okay," I said, looking away to hide my grin. "Then maybe you should lead the Stove Legs."

I couldn't help but smile at Alex's logic. And his verve. I was twenty-two years his senior. I had started climbing before he was born. It wasn't that Alex was disrespectful, but he had no qualms about challenging the status quo. I sensed that I needed to give him more than a cursory explanation of *Look, Alex, this is how I like to do it.*

"Look, Alex, if I put in pro more often, I climb better, I climb faster. It's like a peace-of-mind thing."

He paused, considering the statement. I could almost see his brain sucking in the piece of data, analyzing it against his own experience to determine its validity, and then spitting back out the answer.

"I climb the same regardless," he said.

In twenty-five years of climbing, I had never met anyone quite like Alex. In the end he deferred to my judgment on how many pieces of which gear to bring, at least on our first climb together. We set out in late morning, with one rope and a slightly pared-down rack. The plan was to climb the Nose the way Jim Herson and I had done it in 2001 when we took the record back from Dean and Timmy. I would take the first sixteen pitches, to the King Swing, and Alex would take pitches 17 through 31.

We worked the route like a puzzle, identifying exactly how and when the follower would give the gear he'd cleaned back to the leader. We broke each of our leads roughly in half, to allow for a gear transfer. And we bickered over the finer details like an old married couple.

"Alex, it's easier if you use the bolt ladder on Changing Corners instead of free-climbing it."

"It's no problem for me to free it," he said.

"I get that, but it takes less energy if you use a biner and just pull from bolt to bolt."

"Maybe for you, Hans, but you're a lot older. It doesn't feel any harder to me."

"That's great Alex, the joy of youth. But it's just plain faster to use the bolt ladder."

Even with all the discussion and process reengineering, we topped out in 4:37. I felt pretty good about that.

As we started the hike down, Alex said, "You place gear really fast."

"Is that a compliment or your way of giving me permission to carry up as many #3s as I want?" I asked.

"Neither," Alex said, then broke into a giant grin. "No, both."

As we hiked down, I found out some interesting facts about Alex. He'd had an unusually high GPA in high school, like a 4.7, for excelling in so many advanced classes, but then dropped out of UC Berkeley because he felt like it was a waste of time. He likes to read and enjoys some of the same books I do, including Ayn Rand's *Atlas Shrugged*. Like me, he lost his father too early. And like me, he considers himself an atheist.

Our similarities helped increase my comfort level climbing with him. For atheists, there is no afterlife. This is it, so we tend to *carpe diem*, "seize the day." But we don't do it with reckless abandon. We're very careful with our one life. Barring some crazy accident like Boot Flake peeling off the face of El Capitan, I knew I was safe with Alex.

Over the course of the next two weeks, we continued training, whittling down our time to 3:16, and then 2:37:30—just 45 seconds shy of the record. While it would have been cool to take back the record that year, the winter weather moved in and shut down any further climbing in Yosemite. We agreed to continue our quest in 2012, as soon as the route was dry.

During the winter and spring, I trained indoors at Diablo Rock Gym. As a dad with a full-time job, it was great to have such a strong goal to work for in the spring to improve my fitness level. I was 47 years old, and many of my friends were starting to slow down, exercising less, climbing easier or shorter routes, and getting, well, sedentary. Luckily, I had Alex sending me regular text messages to make sure my "psyche was still high." In other words, to check that I was continuing to bust my butt in the gym.

I also spent some time really dialing in the route in my mind, stripping it down to the exact pieces of gear I'd use on each of my sixteen pitches. I made a list, by pitch, noting each piece I'd need, in the order I'd need it.

And I solicited advice from the experts, including Eric J. Hörst, the foremost authority on climbing fitness and the author of eight books. "You could shave 5 minutes off your time by sleeping at altitude," he told me. I was intrigued but not ready to invest in a hypoxic chamber for my home. Translation: Jacki vetoed it as "ridiculous."

My good friend and coauthor of my speed-climbing book Bill Wright flew out from Colorado to do a reconnaissance climb with me on June 10, before Alex arrived. It was a good way to relieve some stress, scouting the Nose to make sure nothing had changed, and reminding myself of critical points of execution on-route. Most notably, I wanted to make sure I remembered exactly where I needed to place a piece of gear in the thin seam that leads to Boot Flake. There's an exact spot where the cam fits, and if you don't get it right, you end up wasting time fiddling with your pro.

When Alex showed up two days later, I felt comfortably tuned up from my climb with Bill and ready to get to it. Our plan was to attempt the record on Sunday, June 17, which just so happened to be Father's Day and the day before my forty-eighth birthday. Weekends were always best for cheers of support, not only from friends and family but also the media, climbing community supporters, and tourists—the Race for the Nose had become that big of a public spectacle.

Alex and I took a test run up the Nose on June 13 to see where we were at, process-wise and fitness-wise. It took us 2:53. We were still 17 minutes and 8 seconds off the record, but it was an incredible start. On the hike down we brainstormed process improvements.

"I hate carrying gear on my shoulder," Alex said, referring to the sling he wore to clip in the pro he cleaned when following. During my lead, in between pitches 6 and 7, he removed it and handed it back to me. I did the same for him at roughly the halfway point on his lead.

"I could try to make something that you wear around your waist," I suggested. "But it needs to be something you can take off really fast so we don't spend too much time handing over the gear."

"What if we just don't hand over the gear?" Alex asked.

"So I carry enough gear for all sixteen pitches so that I don't need you to replenish me, and you just hold on to the gear you clean?"

"Pretty much."

My initial reaction was "no way." But Alex had earned enough of my respect that I stopped to think about it first. It was certainly possible. And it would remove the two gear handoffs, which were process-time drains on the climb.

"You'd have to pare down your rack, of course," Alex added.

"Of course," I said with a smirk. Alex loved paring down the rack. In reality, I'd have to add some pieces to be able to climb both my leads without having my gear replenished. But that was an argument for later.

"Let's try it," I said.

"How about tomorrow?" Alex asked.

"How about a rest day first?" I answered.

"It will be really good training to climb it while we're tired," Alex said.

"Can you handle it if I'm so tired that it takes us like 6 hours," I asked. Alex rolled his eyes.

"I'm serious," I said. "I need you to be prepared that it might take me that long."

"Yeah, yeah, Hans, whatever." Alex said.

On Thursday we met in the morning and quibbled a bit over the rack. For my 1,600 feet of lead climbing, I had pared it down to sixteen cams, twenty-two quickdraws, three long runners with biners, and eleven free biners. That equates to one piece of pro per every 31 vertical feet—as light and fast as I was willing to go. As we set out, I felt physically beat but mentally amped to try a new method.

On the wall I got a little spooked leading the Stove Legs. It was the one section where I would have liked to have placed more pro. A fall of that length would have most likely ended with a serious injury, and while I'd never fallen on the Stove Legs before, the thought of it made me hesitant to climb at full speed.

When we topped out, I ran hard for the tree, smacked it, and sat down. Alex watched as I pulled my stopwatch off the back of my harness, then pressed a couple buttons to access the main menu to change it from "time of day" mode to "chrono" mode so I could stop the time. "2:39!"

Despite being worn out from having run the vertical marathon up the Nose the day before, we'd done it 14 minutes faster. To use Alex's term, my "psyche level was high" over eliminating the gear handoffs. I could only imagine how fast we could climb the Nose when we were fresh. We were definitely going to set a new record.

But Alex looked upset.

"You know it took you at least 5 seconds to stop the time?" he said, more a statement than a question.

"Well, I switch it to time of day mode after I start it so it doesn't accidentally stop if I bump it while I'm climbing," I explained. "So when we're done, I have to switch it back before I can stop the time."

"Dude, we need to time how long that takes and subtract it," Alex said. He wasn't kidding. And he had a point. In fact, I was kind of surprised I hadn't thought of it. I reset the stopwatch, and we tested how long the fiddling took me: 7 seconds.

"We can deduct 7 seconds on Sunday," I said.

I drove back to the Bay Area and caught up on work. The next day, Friday, I climbed a couple easy 5.10 routes in the gym to stay loose. On Saturday I e-mailed everyone that I thought would care that we were going for the speed record on the Nose. Alex stayed in Yosemite and "recovered" by spending two days backpacking 18 miles in the high country of Tuolumne Meadows. When he came out of the wilderness, he was a bit taken aback by the level of publicity I'd garnered for our record attempt. He called me up, sounding nervous, which was unusual for a climber known among friends as Alex "No Big Deal" Honnold.

"I don't want a lot of people there when we start," he said. "It might mess with my focus."

"But you want them there at the end?" I said.

"Yeah, of course. Whatever," Alex replied.

I paused, trying to come up with a solution or something that would put Alex more at ease.

He spoke before I did. "Can we just tell everyone we're starting at 7 a.m.? Then we'll go early and start at 6 a.m."

I agreed.

The plan didn't exactly work. When we arrived Sunday morning at 5 a.m., about a dozen people were already milling around the meadow. Fortunately, Alex handled it just fine. We started at 5:52 a.m., slightly ahead of schedule.

About two-thirds into my lead, I reached the Stove Legs and summoned my courage. I needed to blast through the hundreds of feet worth of cracks flawlessly and at warp speed, with only minimal gear. As Alex simul-climbed hot on my heels, I concentrated on jamming my hands and feet into the sharp crack, bloodying my ankle in the process. I took only one brief pause to catch my breath, noting that Alex would surely tease me about it later. But it was worth it to lower my heart rate and steady my breathing. There was an updraft in the valley that day, which carried the cheers of the hundreds of people who'd gathered in El Cap Meadow like a breath of fresh air.

When it was my turn to follow Alex, I drew on every last ounce of physical and mental energy to keep up with him. As the follower, I was very aware that I was the one holding the Petzl Grigri, so safety was largely in my hands. Not only was I belaying, but I was climbing at the limit of my cardiovascular ability. By the time I raced up the last pitch to the top, I was dizzy with exhaustion. And elated. I knew without even checking the time that we had the record.

I hit the tree and stopped the watch, subtracting the agreed-upon 7 seconds. I pulled out my phone and called down to Jacki, who was in the meadow with the kids. "2:23:46," I told her. Alex and I had broken Stanley and Dean's record by 12 minutes and 59 seconds.

"I think it can go under 2 hours," Alex said.

"Maybe next year," I said, mostly kidding. "For now, let's enjoy this."

We walked over to the edge of El Capitan so the people in the meadow could see us, standing side by side, our arms raised in a victory V against a cloudless azure-blue sky. The wind pulled the roar of their cheers up to us. I realized then that this was a record that was going to last for a long while. As of the printing of this book in 2016, Alex and my record remains unchallenged.

Afterward, I embraced the Yoda role with new resolve and found it wasn't hard to do. I'd given the speed record on the Nose my absolute best, and finally, I was content. I got in four more Nose ascents that year—all with friends—that ranged from 12 to 38 hours, depending on the experience level and goals of my partners.

Then in 2013 my good friend and climber Will Masterman introduced me to a young British climber named Hazel Findlay who was in town and wanted to climb the Nose. "She's Steve Findlay's daughter—he started taking her outside climbing when she was 7. She's like 20 now," said Will. "She was a six-time junior national rock-climbing champion but gave it all up because she just wanted to do trad outside. She's totally badass."

In my initial phone conservation with Hazel, she seemed to have the right experience and attitude to attempt NIAD. She had one requirement: "I want to climb the entire thing, no jugging."

I was surprised and delighted. No one had ever made that request of me before. I thought it showed a deep reverence for the sport and for El Capitan. Plus, it required a much greater level of strength and skill than the usual method where the leader climbs and the follower jugs. In fact, very few people have the ability to climb *all* of the Nose.

"You got it," I said. "This is going to be really fun."

Initially, I had reservations about how long it would take, with both of us climbing every pitch. Jugging is faster than climbing. To save time, I decided we should lead in blocks instead of switching off every lead. As it turned out, I needn't have worried. Hazel climbed almost as fast as I did, and she was super-efficient with big-wall technique, like handing off gear and switching out belay and general rope management. We topped out in 12:01—my first "jugless ascent."

Later that year Hazel was awarded *Climbing* magazine's Golden Piton Award for trad climbing. Her notable achievements included returning to Yosemite to free-climb Freerider in just three days. My time with her was a reminder that there were still new experiences to be had on the Nose, even for a veteran like me.

The experience also made me think of my own daughter, who was about to turn 12. Mari hadn't shown the same level of interest in climbing that Hazel must have but nonetheless learned at a very young age. When Mari was 9, she became part of the climbing club at the Diablo Rock

Gym, spending two days a week training with a coach and other students her age after school. Mari had even tried a few competitions but didn't stick with it. I hoped we'd climb the Nose together some day.

In June 2015 I made my ninety-ninth ascent of the Nose. It was ideal timing, as Yosemite National Park was celebrating its 125th anniversary that year, and I'd be able to fit in a one hundredth climb in September. I chose Fiona Thornewill as my partner, or rather, she chose me. I met Fiona at a Polish film festival in 2008. She runs Polar Challenge International, a polar expedition company, and was the first British woman to ski to both the North and South Poles. For her fiftieth birthday, Fiona was looking for a unique challenge and had chosen El Capitan. The fact that she holds a speed record to one of the poles sealed the deal for me. As part of her fiftieth-birthday climb, Fiona pledged to raise at least £3,000 for BMC Access & Conservation Trust. She came to the Bay Area in spring 2015 for some initial training and to see if we'd make a good team.

What Fiona lacked in experience on rock, she more than made up for in tenacity and disposition. I told her it was a go. She came back in September, during a stretch of perfect fall weather, and along with adventure journalist Jayme Moye, the coauthor of this book, we sent the Nose in three days and two nights. After doing exclusively NIAD and speed runs for the last decade, and possessing a vanity plate that first read "NOBIVY" and then "LUVNIAD," for me the climb was a fun refresher on the adventure of vertical camping and sleeping on the wall like a mountain goat.

It was also a reminder of how much I enjoyed taking big-wall climbing newbies up the Nose. For my 101th ascent in October, I ran up the Nose with another first-timer: a sport climber friend for twenty years named Marc Heileman. It took us just over 14 hours and was filmed as part of a leadership video series we were helping create.

Shortly after the 101st ascent, Marianna caught me by surprise.

"I was thinking we could climb the Nose, you know, like maybe for my fifteenth birthday?"

She didn't need to ask me twice. I took her to the climbing gym and taught her how to jug, and recruited Will Masterman as our third to help Marianna on the back end of the rope as well as to clean the pro. We drove up to Yosemite the weekend before Thanksgiving break and set out for the base of the Nose bright and early on Sunday, November 22.

We had a fully stocked haul bag good for three nights and two days on the wall and ideal temperatures in the high 60s. I had a blast watching Mari come jugging up after me on the first couple pitches. We took a break at Sickle Ledge, at the top of pitch 4. Mari seemed to be holding up fine, both physically and mentally, and we were making good time to boot. I started to think that maybe we'd only spend one night on the wall.

"Papa?" Mari said.

"Yes, sweetie?"

"I think I'm good," she said.

My heart fell. "I'm good" is Mari-speak for "I'm done now, please."

"You're good?" I asked, just to be sure.

"I'm good," she said.

I tried to smile. "Okay, then let's get off this rock."

As we rappelled back down to the base, it hit me that the first time I'd attempted to climb the Nose, I'd also bailed at Sickle Ledge. I was in college at the time. Mari was only in high school. I smiled. She was way ahead of me.

"I'm really proud of you, honey," I told her, as we rappelled side by side, synchronizing our steps down the smooth granite.

A month later I found out that I'd been selected for induction into the California Outdoor Hall of Fame. My nomination wasn't for holding the speed record on the Nose. It was for a lifelong commitment to climbing, including my one hundredth ascent of the Nose and my efforts in promoting the sport, from running climbing competitions to working with junior climbers, to exposing more people to Yosemite, to guiding disabled climbers up El Cap.

These days I get hired to speak to audiences—at corporations, conferences, trade shows, universities, Rotary clubs, and small businesses—all over the world about climbing. As I say in those talks, what I do does not save lives in Africa or get kids off the street in America's ghettos, yet I'm passionate about it. And apparently sharing that passion has a ripple effect. Many people, months or years after hearing my story, have approached me to say thanks. One person told me he found the courage to accept a job in China, which led to incredible life experiences and adventures. Another was inspired to begin working with Doctors Without Borders, another to leave an unsatisfying job to travel the world, and still another to commit to a trip to trek in Nepal in between corporate jobs.

Why on earth would anyone climb the Nose one hundred times (or 101 times, as of the date of this publishing)? I'm not sure that's the right question. How about this one: Why on earth would anyone work a job they don't care about, day after day, for 261 days a year, every year? Or this one: Why would someone who has a choice settle for "good enough" instead of going after great?

One of my favorite books is Jim Collins's *Good to Great*. It talks about how corporations let good stand in the way of great. Jim just so happens to be a climber. When he set out to climb the Nose, he went for NIAD, and he climbed the whole thing—no jugging. That's not just good, that's great. Or as my coauthor Jayme says, "follow the heat," which is another way of saying find your passion, your "Precious." Mine is El Capitan and specifically, the Nose route up El Capitan. For all of my adult life, I've been either directly or indirectly putting my energy into climbing that route, to the absolute best of my ability. It was a risky investment, riskier than say, building a career at Parker Seals, but the return has been huge. In a way, I can tie everything and everyone I love most in life back to the Nose. And the dividends are still coming. My next challenge is to climb El Capitan 200 times. I'm at 161, and yes, most of those have been the Nose. I wouldn't have it any other way.

On belay, climb on.

Appendix A

Hans's Logbook of Nose Ascents

1. July 1989, Mike Lopez, 46 hours
My first Nose ascent was with Mike, a college buddy on the track-and-field team. It took us two tries. Our first attempt, the year prior, was an epic fail and we bailed after 12 hours on the fourth pitch. It's worth noting that Mike was a fellow pole-vaulter—the only endeavor more ridiculous than climbing.

2. May 1990, Steve Schneider, 8:05 (record)
I set my first speed record on the Nose with Steve, who asked me to call him Shipoopi. At the time, Shipoopi was the best all-around El Cap climber in addition to one of my idols. He soon became my best friend. Today, he possesses one of the most badass El Cap résumés on the planet (see Speedclimb.com for the others).

3. June 1991, Andres Puhvel, 6:03 (record)
Andy was just a college kid when we set this record. We'd been competitors on the local climbing-comp scene, trading off wins in difficulty. He never did best me in a speed event . . . well, once, at his local crag. When we got to the top of the Nose, we were floored when we looked at the watch—we never thought we could do better than the immortals Dave Schultz and Peter Croft.

4. June 1991, Andres Puhvel, 6:17
Andy and I climbed the Nose again, just in case we could do it even faster.
We couldn't.

5. August 1991, Nancy Feagin, 10:05 (male-female record)
Nancy was a climber before we met and my girlfriend at the time of the
climb. I remember being stunned at her climbing talent. She went on to
win many climbing competitions, guide at an expert level in the Tetons,
and even summit Mount Everest while nursing a lung infection.

6. May 1992, Kevin Thaw, 6:01
Kevin is a true all-around master of the sport. I always thought he was
so hard-core because he could wield ice tools one month and crush hard
sport-climbing routes the next. And because he has a British accent.

7. June 1992, Peter Croft, 4:22 (record)
I'll never forget how excited I was to get to climb with Peter Croft, who
was already a legend in his own time. Or how, shortly into the climb, he
ripped off his shirt. The guy sent the Nose in just a pair of shorts.

8. July 1992, Lynn Hill, 8:40 (male-female record)
Lynn was doing reconnaissance to free-climb the Nose. I was psyched
to get to climb with her; she was already considered one of the greatest
climbers on earth. It was the first time I climbed the Nose with a professional photographer and rigger present.

9. July 1993, Nancy Feagin, 9:52
This climb was the start of our "20 classic climbs in 20 days" adventure,
along with Christian Santelices and Willie Benegas. Nancy had broken
up with me shortly before, but our ascent proved that climbing the Nose

is so remarkable that it's possible to have a good time even with your ex-girlfriend.

10. August 1993, myself, 14:11 (solo record)
I had knee surgery to have a torn meniscus removed and the doc said not to do anything strenuous for at least ten days. Ten days later I did my first roped-solo ascent. Maybe I should have waited longer—my knee swelled to the size of a small volleyball.

11. May 1994, Steve Schneider, Craig Cleveland, Jim Soash, 52 hours
A fund-raising climb for Access Fund (a national advocacy organization that keeps US climbing areas open and conserves the climbing environment), Craig and Jim were the highest bidders. It was the second time that I climbed the Nose with Shipoopi, who possessed ten times the knowledge I did with regard to big-wall techniques, so I learned a lot.

12. June 1994, Ben Ditto, Jake Slaney, Jody Evans, 16:24 (four-person team record)
I think of this as the climb of youthful ignorance (mine). I took these guys up simply because it was a challenge. I'd never met Jody before—for all I knew, this was his first climb. Jake had never been more than a pitch up any route, and it was probably a sport route. Ben had ten or fewer total trad pitches under his belt. To make things even more difficult, we agreed that each team member had to lead at least one pitch. Despite the odds, it was the first four-person NIAD ascent. Heck, it might be the only one.

13. June 1994, Steve Schneider, 6:28
At the time, this climb was a huge deal for me because it was my first linkup of two big-wall routes. We started with the Nose and then climbed Steck-Salathé after. I remember feeling really happy. And really tired.

14. July 1994, Kathleen Laskey, 33 hours

Shipoopi introduced me to this wonderful woman, a climber of endless energy. She and I started dating and decided to take a run up the Nose together. It was her first time.

15. August 1994, Marina McClean, 41 hours

Marina was my first girlfriend, from back in my college days in the 1980s. We had stayed friends afterward and remained in touch. She's one of the many great people in the outdoor community that I feel fortunate to have spent quality time with on the Nose.

16. August 1994, Rossano Boscarino, 12:28

Rossano and I met through PMI/Petzl. He was a caver who held two world records in mechanical vertical rope climbing. Climbing the Nose got him hooked on big-wall climbing, and he promised he'd be back. True to his word, Rossano returned to Yosemite to climb with me in 2003 and again in 2004. He runs a guiding company called Aventuras Tierra Adentro based in San Juan, Puerto Rico.

17. August 1994, Pascal and Eugene Berger, 29:45

Oddly, both of these two could out-sport-climb me any day. They were friends of Lynn Hill's from Belgium. They had a nanny watching their kid in an RV and were psyched to go up the best route in the world as fast as possible, and then get back to playing with their kid. They weren't concerned with the "style" of the ascent—whether they jugged or led or free-climbed. They just wanted to scale the greatest rock in the world. Their attitude opened my eyes to the ridiculousness of people getting hung up on the style of ascent. If a route is good, then it's worth doing. Who cares if you jug some of it, or all of it, or free-climb it, or French free-climb it? Just do it.

18. October 1994, Steve Schneider, 5:42
Shipoopi and I climbed the Nose to kick off a project we dubbed the "El Cap Trifecta." The idea was to climb three routes on El Cap—the Nose, Lurking Fear, and the West Face—in a day. I was thrilled that we not only accomplished it, but also set a new speed record on Lurking Fear, in 8:52. I remember getting to the top of the Nose and walking over to Lurking Fear and rappelling down it, much to the surprise of a team of three who were on their way up, and setting up a portaledge for the evening. We passed them again about 4 hours later while we were climbing back up in the dark. They were like, *What the heck are you guys doing?*

19. July 1995, Steve Schneider, Jon Williams, 40 hours
What a delight to get to climb the Nose with my best friend as a fund-raiser for the Access Fund. This time, Jon was the highest bidder, and we all spent two great days on the route.

20. August 1995, Neal Florine, 31 hours
For my twentieth Nose ascent, I climbed with my younger brother, Neal. Perhaps more naturally gifted than myself or our older brother Keith, Neal could off-the-couch climb hard 5.10s and best both of us in tennis, despite spending far less time on the court.

21. September 1995, Martin Laulxes, 11:22
Martin and I met at Camp 4 and got along really well, so we decided to head up the best route in the world together. I figured, heck, he's European, we need to show visitors a good time.

22. November 1995, Mark Melvin, 8:03
Journalist Eileen Hansen was writing an article about me for *Sports Illustrated*, and a trip to Yosemite, complete with a Nose climb, seemed in

order. My friend Mark, who is also the founder along with his wife Debra of the largest climbing-gym company in the United States, Touchstone Climbing Inc., was game. I've done a ton of climbing with Mark on El Capitan (and other granite cliffs), and three times, he's helped me train to get the speed record on the Nose. I'd vote him most likely to be a Nose speed record holder, if only he were interested in such things.

23. August 1996, Steve Schneider, Tom Isaacson, 36 hours
Another fund-raiser for the Access Fund. Tom was an especially competent and hospitable character and would go on to climb other big-wall routes with both Steve and me.

24. August 1996, Erik Weihenmayer, Sam Bridgem, Jeff Evans, 60+ hours
I joined Erik and his team for the first blind ascent of El Capitan. When people ask me which of my Nose climbs have been the most memorable, I always think of this one first.

25. June 1997, Yuji Hirayama, Kenji Iiyama, 50+ hours
This was a pretty darn interesting climb. There I was, with the best on-sight trad free climber in the world, on the best route in the world, doing reconnaissance for free climbing it. In the end, we were able to free all but 15 feet of the Great Roof and 15 feet of the Changing Corners pitch. And although Kenji is known for being on the eyepiece end of the camera, I came to find that he could out-climb me when given the chance.

26. July 1997, Yuji Hirayama, 32+ hours
After a day of rest, Yuji went back up to do more free-climbing reconnaissance to see if it could go in a single push. His prognosis: "I think it would go, but it would be hard."

27. August 1997, Greg Murphy, 5:37

Greg has been climbing, and climbing in Yosemite, for much longer than me. He is unflappable, under even the most adverse conditions. Most notably, Greg is super-capable of long pushes, which includes long drives before and after climbs, to and from the San Francisco Bay Area (a skill that cannot be overemphasized when you are transitioning into the world of being of a responsible adult, having kids, and trying to keep a regular, paying job).

28. September 1997, Chad Nichols, 10:20

Chad seemed to be at the cutting edge of all the fun new emerging sports. He was an ace at windsurfing early on and later, kite surfing. I met him at Mission Cliffs climbing gym, and he said he wanted to do NIAD, so we went.

29. July 1998, Nancy Feagin, 9:35

I climbed the Nose with Nancy as part of her project to become the first woman to do the Half Dome–El Capitan linkup. She did it in a day, a feat that went unrepeated for ten years.

30. June 1999, Chandlee Harrell, 7:40

Chandlee was a fellow climber at nearly the same place on the path as me (recently getting married, having kids, holding down a job). We did this climb shortly after my second knee surgery, to remove the meniscus on the knee that hadn't gotten its turn four years prior. I think I waited more than ten days after the surgery to climb, but I can't be sure. What I remember most is the fact that we passed nine parties on the route, so many that it started to become humorous (and I believe a record number for me).

31. July 24, 1999, myself, 13:40
I know the exact date of this one because I committed to it publicly, on my website, as part of an attempt to become the first person to rope-solo Half Dome and El Capitan in less than a day. Dean Potter ended up beating me to it, but still, it was my biggest day of climbing ever. I remember being intimidated by the Half Dome hike, so I climbed that one first, in the morning. I finished the Nose at 2:30 a.m. and was completely knackered.

32. October 1999, Alard Hufner, 9:23
Alard was a climber from South Africa. He had previously hiked to the top of both Half Dome and El Cap to photograph me during the roped-solo linkup, making him possibly the first person to rappel off the top of the Nose before actually climbing it. He may also be the first South African to have done NIAD.

33. March 2000, Jacqueline Adams, Beth Rodden, 3 days
The first time my then-future wife Jacki and I climbed the Nose together! She originally said she wouldn't do it with me because it would be like "cheating." But I was able to convince her to come as a mentor for Beth, whom we knew from the climbing gym and who was only 20 at the time. Beth went on to combine her extraordinary sport-climbing skills with big-wall and trad tenacity to become one of the most well-known free climbers in the climbing world.

34. May 27, 2000, Steve Schneider, 5:46
It was Shipoopi's fortieth birthday—what better way to celebrate than taking a run up the Nose? He had wanted to climb forty pitches in a day

for his fortieth, and the Nose is only thirty-two, so he went and climbed the Nutcracker with his friend Jenny afterward.

35. July 31, 2000, Peter Coward, 7:12
Peter was in the "work a regular job in the city category," but you'd never know it by how quickly and competently he moved on the rock. We'd partnered on other routes on El Cap before, doing some really long pushes, but this was our first time on the Nose together. We timed our total trip, including drive time from the Bay Area and back, and coined the phrase "Nose in a Day from the Bay." A friend, Kristi Denton Cohen, was making a documentary on the history of Yosemite climbing and shot some footage of us. Her resulting film, *Vertical Frontier*, won multiple awards, including "Best Film on Climbing" at the 2002 Banff Mountain Film Festival.

36. June 18, 2001, Sue Hartley-Etter, 2 days
Sue was a longtime climber on the East Coast scene who'd always wanted to do the Nose. She was a joyful climber, and I really enjoyed partnering with her.

37. September 5–9, 2001, Beth Rodden, Scott Cory, Tori Allen, Steve Schneider, Tommy Caldwell, Rob Raker, 4 days
The infamous *Wall Rats* ascent—nothing less then a Beach Blanket Babylon on the vertical walls of El Capitan. Watch the film for all the funny details (Wallrats.com).

38. September 2001, Tommy Caldwell, 4:31 minutes
Had I not been coughing up a lung, feverish, and backed off a lead to hand it over to Tommy, we surely would have broken Peter Croft's and

my record time of 4:22. Tommy is an incredible climber. He went on to free-climb "the Hardest Free Climb in the World," located next door to the Nose, on the Dawn Wall. He has also proven his ability to move fast in epic places like Patagonia. I'm really glad I went out climbing with him despite not feeling well.

39. October 23, 2001, Jacqueline Florine, Chelsea Rude, 38 hours
Chelsea was a teenager at the time, an up-and-comer on the competition circuit with an adventurous spirit. I was only too happy to, along with my wife, introduce Chelsea to big-wall trad climbing. I remember we bivied on El Cap Tower, my favorite ledge to sleep on.

40. October 28, 2001, Jim Herson, 3:57 (record)
I wanted to reclaim the speed record on the Nose. Jim wanted to practice free climbing the Salathé Headwall next door. We combined forces by climbing the Nose fast in order to get to the top of El Capitan so we could walk over to the Salathé and set up a toprope so Jim could spend the rest of the day working out free-climbing moves on the headwall. He tells the story way better than I do—Jim's self-deprecating sense of humor is highly regarded in our local climbing community. Follow him on Facebook and you'll see.

41. March 20, 2002, Jacqueline Florine, Harry Pali, 2 days
Sometimes deciding to climb the Nose comes down to meeting a big, lovable character at the gym that you can't resist. Harry isn't your quintessential climber—his build is more akin to that of a Samoan construction worker (which he was)—but he dreamed of climbing El Capitan just the same. He committed for his fiftieth birthday, and Jacki and I were delighted to make the ascent with him.

42. June 3, 2002, Mark Melvin, 14:10
My coauthor of *Speed Climbing*, Bill Wright, was going for NIAD, so Mark and I went up to capture the ascent with photos and video. I still use the footage in my speed-climbing presentations.

43. June 18, 2002, Jim Thornburg, 4 days
Jim and I climbed the Nose in order to film and photograph Jacki on her quest to become the first woman to rope-solo the Nose. I can't say I climbed it *with* her because she refused all contact of any kind. Jim and I camped on top the last night so we could watch her finish the next morning—a memory that still gives me goose bumps.

44. July 2002, Mark Gain, 10:30
Mark and I met through a mutual friend in the climbing community who suggested that we team up for his NIAD attempt. As evidenced by our fast time, this was not Mark's first time on the Nose.

45. September 4, 2002, Scott Bovard, Garreth Miller, 3 days
Scott and Garreth are both buddies of mine from the local climbing gym community. When not on the wall, Scott works in real estate and shares my penchant for reading business self-help books like *Good to Great*, *The 4-Hour Workweek*, and *Focal Point*. Garreth is a firefighter. During this climb we experienced the worst conditions I've ever seen on El Cap. The day began normally, with 70°F temps, then a cold front moved in, dropping the temperature nearly 40 degrees and dousing us in freezing rain and sleet. We made the best of it. I couldn't have asked for two better partners to literally weather the storm.

46. September 23, 2002, Yuji Hirayama, 3:27
Ostensibly, I talked Yuji into a speedy Nose ascent as part of his visit to
Yosemite to free-climb the Salathé. I was surprised at how fast we went.
And Yuji was so psyched about our time that he agreed to make a formal
bid for the record with me the following week.

47. September 29, 2002, Yuji Hirayama, 2:48:55 (record)
"Pleasantly shocked" was how I felt about this record-setting climb. It
was my first sub-3-hour ascent on the Nose. It was also the first arrival
of an "organized crowd" to witness the spectacle of the speed record on
the Nose.

48. June 12, 2003, Austin Matulonis, 14:10
Austin was a member at Pipeworks climbing gym in Sacramento. The
manager up there, Vaughn Medford, connected us, saying we'd be a good
match for NIAD. Austin worked as a California highway patrolman, and
our climb landed me in the CHP magazine. (Thanks Vaughn! And when
are you going to climb the Nose with me?)

49. June 22, 2003, Stein Skaar, Scott Bovard, 15:52
Stein was the manager of Berkeley Ironworks at the time, one of the
climbing gyms in the Touchstone family, so we worked together. Funny,
I'm pretty sure we just kind of snuck out of work, got in a NIAD, then
drove back to the bay.

50. June 25, 2003, Rossano Boscarino, 12:41
After climbing the Nose with me nine years prior, my caver friend Rossano from Puerto Rico returned to have another go at it. He was successful in achieving his goal of leading half of the pitches.

51. June 30, 2003, Dick Duane, Randy Spurier, 3 days
Both Dick and Randy are prominent figures in the Bay Area climbing community. Dick is the lawyer who helped persuade the Park Service to designate Camp 4 as a historic monument so that it did not get plowed under for apartments. Randy helped launch Super Topo. Dick was 64 at the time we climbed the Nose, and I remember he led the Great Roof, perhaps the oldest person ever to do so.

52. August 19, 2003, Ken Karas, Richard Frank, Rob Raker, Steve Schneider, 3 days
Ken and Richard were enthusiastic adventurers that I met through the Young Presidents Organization. They got us to produce a film on their ascent of the Nose. Similar to *Wall Rats*, it was really fun to do a vertical camping–style ascent with a small group.

53. September 2003, Mark Cartier, 14:00
Mark Kroese, the author of *Fifty Favorite Climbs*, introduced me to Mark Cartier. Soon after, we set a date to climb NIAD. Mark was a super-competent partner.

54. May 30, 2004, Peter Coward, 7:49
Peter turned 40 a couple weeks before me, so we did this as our combined birthday climb. Afterward, we climbed the Regular Northwest Face of Half Dome for the highly lauded linkup. I've been fortunate to climb many routes around the valley with Peter. Only Shipoopi, Yuji, and my wife have climbed El Capitan with me more times than Peter.

55. July 13, 2004, John Georgevits, 14:50
At the time, John was an East Coaster whom I met through the competition-climbing community. Now he lives in California. I contributed

to his book *The Best Use of a Lifetime*. We share an appreciation for similar philosophical and physical endeavors.

56. September 20, 2004, Rossano Boscarino, 11:06
For Rossano's third visit to the valley, he aspired to do the Half Dome–El Cap linkup. We climbed Half Dome first, followed by the Nose. It was my fourth time doing the linkup.

57. May 12, 2005, Jim Cope, Rich Fettke, Jacqueline Florine, 3 days
Jim is a friend and fellow parent in the East Bay climbing community. We did this climb in celebration of his fiftieth birthday. Rich is a friend and mentor, a body builder turned motivational speaker, whom I also met at the climbing gym. Coincidentally, Rich and I both competed in the inaugural X Games in Rhode Island in 1995, he in bungee jumping, me in speed climbing, but we didn't know each other then.

58. July 16, 2005, Ron Ause, 3 days
Ron hails from Arizona and needed to go out of state in order to climb a taller cliff. I really enjoyed climbing with him—a fun, positive climbing partner. Also of note: I've spent a good bit of time in Arizona, in and around Phoenix but more so in Tucson with my buddy Jason Mullins, who has yet to climb the Nose with me (hint).

59. September 19, 2005, Rich Fettke, Dan Herz, 16:02
Dan was a television producer from San Francisco. He had little climbing experience but became intrigued with the idea of climbing El Cap after covering a few TV journalism pieces on climbing that I was involved with. It took us two attempts—the first time was in the summer, and we ran out of water about halfway up due to extreme heat and bailed. Our second run went far better.

60. September 23, 2005, Bob Yoho, 13:31
At the time, I think Bob and I were the "oldest team" to climb NIAD, at 51 and 41 years old, respectively. Also of note, Bob enjoyed tinkering with climbing techniques and came up with a useful way to simul-climb that kept both climbers totally on belay. He called it the "Yo-Go Method," a blend of his name with that of his coinventor, Chris Gonzales.

61. June 16, 2006, Peter Darmi, 14:11
I've known Peter since the early 1990s when the first national climbing competitions started happening in the United States. Peter shared my love of pushing the sport, organizing competitions, and getting in loads of climbing in a single day. Our ascent became the reigning "oldest" NIAD—at the time I was 42 and he was 57.

62. June 24, 2006, Wayne Willoughby, Tico, 22:00
Wayne was an old friend of Shipoopi's who had become an accomplished climber despite suffering from the late effects of paralytic polio and post-polio syndrome. We'd made three other ascents on El Cap together before taking on the Nose, along with Tico, who was renting a room at my Yosemite house at the time. Wayne's ascent marked the first NIAD by an adaptive climber.

63. September 2006, myself, 11:41 (record)
With the exception of the roped-solo record, which I'd lost in 1999 when Dean Potter took it under 13 hours, I had all the speed records on the Nose, including the fastest team time (both male-female and male-male), fastest three-person, and fastest four-person. I decided I wanted to recapture the solo record. I remember it was tough—I had to pass four parties and even helped tow up a rope for three pitches for a team that had been

on the wall for three days already and only had a liter of water left (and likely had two more days of climbing to go).

64. October 21, 2007, Mark Melvin, 8:35
I had just returned from Europe, where I'd gotten an e-mail from Alex Huber that they'd set a new speed record on the Nose, and I wanted to try a speedy ascent to see if I still had a shot at the record. Mark was willing and able. This was our warm-up for climb no. 65.

65. November 2007, Mark Melvin, 5:29
After this climb I felt confident that I could be a contender to reclaim the speed record. I asked Mark if he wanted to make a formal bid for the record with me. He humbly declined. Yuji was coming back for the 2008 season, so I made it through the winter by dreaming of the spring.

66. May 31, 2008, Steve Fettke, 14:00
Steve was my good friend Rich's brother. He came in from the greater Sacramento area to do a birthday climb.

67. June 7, 2008, Carl Page, 16:40
Carl contacted me from Salt Lake City and told me he was turning 50 and looking for a challenge. I agreed that the Nose was a fitting endeavor.

68. June 16, 2008, Mark Melvin, 7:59
Yuji was coming to town, and in preparation Mark climbed the Nose with me for a tune-up.

69. June 23, 2008, Yuji Hirayama, 4:48
Yuji and I did a test run one day after he got off the plane from Japan. The *San Francisco Chronicle* put us on the front page of the paper the next day.

70. June 26, 2008, Yuji Hirayama, 3:28:55
I headed back to the bay for a couple days for work, then Yuji and I climbed the Nose for test run no. 2. The *San Francisco Chronicle* covered us again.

71. June 29, 2008, Yuji Hirayama, 2:47:30
Test run no. 3. I felt good about our time—it was our personal best up to that point. We were ready.

72. July 2, 2008, Yuji Hirayama, 2:43:33 (record)
This climb vies with the Erik Weihenmayer ascent as the most memorable. Thanks to all the local press, we had a huge supportive crowd in the meadow. They didn't know our finish time because we'd gone out of sight when we crested the summit. We radioed down the result, and the cheers and roars carried all the way up.

73. August 2, 2008, Margaret and Paul Hara, Sarah Land, Humberto Marquez, Steve Schneider, 3 days
These are all neighborhood friends of mine and Jacki's. Paul and Humberto started two days before the rest of us. We caught them at the halfway point, and all six of us finished the climb together.

74. September 29, 2008, Yuji Hirayama, 4:07
Even though Yuji and I had already reclaimed the speed record, this was the timing that he'd worked out with a Japanese film crew for a prime-time news segment. So we went at it again.

75. October 5, 2008, Yuji Hirayama, 3:37
Test run no. 2.

76. October 8, 2008, Yuji Hirayama, 2:48:23
Test run no. 3.

77. October 12, 2008, Yuji Hirayama, 2:37:05 (record)
It was a chilly fall morning for our record run. A record crowd gathered
in the meadow. Eric Perlman captured the climb for the film *Masters of
Stone VI*. In the end, Yuji and I shaved another 6 minutes and 28 seconds
off the speed record on the Nose. It was the only time I've ever beaten my
own record on the Nose.

78. July 4, 2009, Mike Lopez, 14:11
My first climbing partner on the Nose, Mike came to Yosemite to climb
it again with me exactly twenty years later. We reduced our original ascent
time of 46 hours by nearly 70 percent. But who's counting?

79. September 7, 2009, Tom Lambert, 14:00
My neighbor in Yosemite West, Tom is an under-the-radar superstar. He
can outrun, outski, and out–wheelbarrow race me. He said it was cheating
to do NIAD with me but that cheating on some things in life isn't so bad.

80. May 7, 2010, Brian Gallant, 13:32
I invited Brian, a fun and enthusiastic friend from the speed-climbing
competition circuit, to come visit and climb NIAD with me, and he took
me up on it.

81. May 21, 2010, Tim Felton, 12:31
Tim was a fellow Access Fund supporter and an advocate for taking
youths into the mountains.

82. June 13, 2011, Lisa Coleman, 14:00

I'd known Lisa for seventeen years at the time; we'd climbed big walls together in the late 1990s but never the Nose. I also attended her wedding—she married Andy Puhvel.

83. June 15, 2011, Craig DeMartino, 12:57

Craig and I were strangers when he first e-mailed me in 2005. He wrote that he was just getting back into climbing following a year of recovery after a climbing accident in Colorado that shattered both his feet and ankles, broke his back and neck, tore his rotator cuff, cracked his ribs, and punctured his right lung. His right leg was so destroyed that he'd opted to have it amputated. Craig had read about a disabled-climbing competition in Florida and was hoping to enter. He was wondering if I had any advice to offer on speed climbing. I told him to give me a call. We talked for a while, and I was so impressed by his resolve that I invited him to come climb in Yosemite with me. He came the following season, in 2006, arriving with his wife and two kids. We climbed Lurking Fear in 14 hours, making Craig the first amputee to send El Cap in a day. We've been friends ever since. In 2011 we climbed NIAD. Craig made me realize that there's really no plausible excuse for *not* climbing.

84. October 13, 2011, Alex Honnold, 4:37

Alex is one in a million. His perspective on life is unique and refreshing. I think he's the only person I've ever met who wanted to go even faster and lighter on the Nose than I did. This was our first climb together, and it was a test run to set a new speed record on the Nose.

85. October 20, 2011, Alex Honnold, 3:16:30
Test run no. 2. For these test runs, I had to drive up the night before, or the morning of, at some ungodly hour. My friend Will Masterman helped out with the driving so that I could sleep en route (thanks again, buddy). Sometimes it takes a village to be a big-wall climber and hold down a regular job.

86. November 1, 2011, Alex Honnold, 2:37:30
Test run no. 3. I remember thinking how amazing it was that we were only 45 seconds shy of the record after having done just two previous climbs together. Unfortunately, the winter weather moved in and put an end to our efforts for the 2011 season.

87. June 10, 2012, Bill Wright, 10:50
At the start of the 2012 Yosemite climbing season, my friend Bill was generous enough to come out from Colorado so I could do a brush-up climb before starting my next round of practice runs with Alex.

88. June 13, 2012, Alex Honnold, 2:53
Test run no. 1. I felt relieved over our fast time—it meant I'd managed to maintain a high fitness level during my time away from Yosemite during the winter and spring. It was probably just "no big deal" for Alex.

89. June 14, 2012, Alex Honnold, 2:39
Test run no. 2. I didn't think that speed climbing the Nose on back-to-back days was a great idea. Alex thought differently, so I gave it a try. The fact that we ended up climbing the Nose only 3 minutes off the record, with no rest, gave me the confidence that our upcoming record attempt on Sunday could potentially be incredibly fast.

90. June 17, 2012, Alex Honnold, 2:23:46 (record)

We got the speed record on the Nose on the day before my forty-eighth birthday, which was also Father's Day. Best present ever.

91. July 14, 2012, Will Masterman, Jeannette Renneberg, 15:00

I'll never say no to NIAD. Especially one coordinated by two of my friends.

92. September 6, 2012, Steve Smith, 12:00

Steve was another connection from Arizona and a highly competent climber—we put up a really respectable NIAD time.

93. October 14, 2012, David Dailey, 38 hours

I have been a performer and rigger for the vertical dance troop Bandaloop since 1991 (that's a whole other story). David was a climber who was on Bandaloop's board, as well as a big supporter of the organization. It was great fun to climb the Nose with someone whom I work with in the "art world."

94. October 16, 2012, Mike Ruckhaus, 27 hours

Another fund-raiser for the Access Fund. Mike was a really solid climber from Alaska looking to get some big-wall experience.

95. October 30, 2013, Hazel Findlay, 12:01

Hazel, a British citizen, was just 20 years old at the time, but as Steve Findlay's daughter, she had over a decade of climbing experience under her belt. At her request, we made my first "jugless" ascent of the Nose, which means the follower climbs each pitch after the leader (instead of the typical method where the follower jugs the rope using ascenders).

Hazel was a delight to climb and adventure with, and I believe fewer than twenty people have done this style of NIAD.

96. May 30, 2014, Peter Coward, 8:31

Just like we did for our fortieth birthdays, Peter and I climbed the Nose together for our fiftieth. We did it about an hour slower, because, well, you know. We also skipped Half Dome that afternoon. Fun fact: Peter is one of the rare people I've climbed with who is taller than I am (I'm 6 feet 1 inch).

97. June 8, 2014, Julie Spiker, 30 hours

I've known Julie for over twenty years through the Bay Area climbing community. She works as an instructor at Diablo Rock Gym. I'm not sure if she considered it an employee perk or a punishment to ascend her first big wall with her boss.

98. June 19, 2015, James Williams, Will Masterman, 14:01

James is a huge supporter of Bandaloop and an accomplished climber from Texas. We initially thought we'd go up for the traditional multiday ascent, but James was so fast that we ended up doing NIAD.

99. June 29, 2015, Stas Yurkevich, 14:30

Stas is a local Bay Area climber who pushes the limit with me on climbing challenges in the gym. He's also an avid supporter of the Access Fund and Yo Basecamp, which is Andy Puhvel's organization dedicated to teaching kids about outdoor climbing.

100. September 12, 2015, Fiona Thornewill, Jayme Moye, 3 days

For my one hundredth, I wanted to do something special. I became friends with Fiona, a polar explorer from the United Kingdom, at a Polish film festival in 2008. Fiona was turning 50 and wanted to do an epic adventure and a fund-raiser, so we combined forces. Adventure journalist Jayme Moye accompanied us, as part of her research to cowrite this book. It was Jayme's first big wall, and I remember standing on a ledge with her on the second day when she noticed a "mist" in the air. I had to explain that a climber above was taking a leak.

101. October 30, 2015, Marc Heileman, 13:57
Once I hit one hundred Nose ascents, I started working toward 200 total El Cap ascents. This climb with Marc put me at 161. We'd known each other for twenty years through sport-climbing competitions and exchanging ideas on climbing as a team-building exercise. As part of this climb, we were shooting footage for a corporate leadership program.

Appendix B

Firsts

First ascent: Warren Harding, Wayne Merry, and George Whitmore; November 12, 1958. Took thirty-three days of "prep work" and twelve days for the final push.

First single-push ascent: Tom Frost, Joe Fitschen, Chuck Pratt, and Royal Robbins; 1960. Took seven days. This was also the second ascent of the route.

First solo ascent: Tom Bauman; 1969

First Nose in a Day (NIAD) ascent: Jim Bridwell, John Long, and Billy Westbay; 1975

First NIAD solo: Steve Schneider; 1989

First female NIAD: Nancy Feagin and Sue McDevitt; 1992

First free ascent: Lynn Hill; 1993

First female solo ascent: Jacki Adams Florine; 2002

Fastest male ascent: Alex Honnold and Hans Florine; 2012, 2:23:46

Fastest female ascent: Chantel Astorga and Mayan Smith-Gobat; 2013, 4:43

Appendix C

The Nose by the Numbers

Number of times Hans has climbed the Nose: 101

Number of people Hans has climbed the Nose with: 87

Number of days Hans has been on the Nose: 189

Number of times Hans has bailed off the Nose: 11

Number of pitches climbed on the Nose by Hans: 3,350

Number of times Hans has rappelled the Nose: 1

Youngest partner on the Nose: 11

Oldest partner on the Nose: 64

Gallons of water brought up by Hans: 420

Number of parties passed on the Nose: 183

Number of times been passed on the Nose: 24

Number of times Hans has bivied on the Nose: 39

Number of times Hans has climbed El Capitan: 161

Number of miles climbed on El Capitan: 92

Number of items dropped off the Nose by Hans: 102

TOP CLIMBING PARTNERS

Climber	Number of Times Climbed El Capitan with Hans / Climbed the Nose with Hans
Steve Schneider	22/10
Yuji Hirayama	14/12
Jacki Adams Florine	10/4
Peter Coward	9/3
Mark Melvin	7/5
Andres Puhvel	6/2
Alex Honnold	6/6
Greg Murphy	5/1

ACKNOWLEDGMENTS

I could not have had the opportunity to "be a climber" without the open-mindedness of my mom and dad. I went to college, got a degree, took a yuppie job, and then I turned from that path and became a full-time climber. The support from Maryann and Thomas Florine, whether I was climbing a tree, selling vegetables from a wagon, pole vaulting, painting fences, hammering nails, studying, not studying, managing a production facility in downtown Los Angeles, or living out of a van, was unwavering. Thank you.

My wife, Jacki Adams Florine, has climbed the Nose with me four times, and El Cap ten times. Climbing big walls is hard, but giving birth to two humans, staying happily married to me, raising two kids (three, counting me), managing our household, and accomplishing audacious goals of her own (like running the Badwater Ultramarathon) is something above and beyond "hard." There are no words for how much I love, respect, and appreciate this woman.

The climbing and outdoor community has provided me with an enormous amount of support, and the long list of individuals, organizations, and companies is only partially represented in this book. I would like to call out one climber, Steve Schneider, whose impact on me was so great that I'm certain he changed my climbing path. From the get-go, I loved competing and I loved sport climbing. Steve was exceptional at both, while also having a very strong background in trad (traditional) and big-wall climbing. He took me under his wing in that arena, inviting me on adventures as if we had been climbing for a decade together. His fun-loving character is perhaps best described as highly competent, yet highly serious only when he needs to be. Steve has no equal in his diverse accomplishments in climbing. What path did he set me on? The path to 101 ascents of the Nose. Had he not shown me that the Nose could be not only completed, but enjoyed, in 8 hours, it's highly probable that I would never have climbed it again. Perhaps not even climbed El Capitan again.

I'm also very fortunate to be part of the close-knit community of climbers at Diablo Rock Gym, which I manage, and the greater Touchstone Climbing family. Our motto at DRG is "Do hard things," and the super-positive folks there have enabled some of my most rewarding climbing adventures to date. I love "working" with all of you.

As for the art of writing, I must acknowledge John Burbidge and Bill Wright. More than ten years ago, they got me my first book deal to write *Climb On*, which later, in its second edition, became *Speed Climbing*. Without John and Bill's encouragement, I may not have committed to speed climbing big walls—which has served me so well in my climbing career and been the foundation for so many of the stories for this book— or to writing, something I've found takes even more courage than climbing. Thank you also to Max Phelps with Globe Pequot/Falcon Guides, who has always been there with a "Yes, Hans, we can do that."

My editor at Falcon, Dave Costello, was diplomatic in "heavily suggesting" that I partner with a coauthor on this narrative. Dave's wisdom in directing me and Jayme, from subtle nuances to overall story structure, was always spot-on. I am grateful for all his talents, especially his ability to let us run loose while somehow keeping us moving toward what you have read here.

An extra-special thanks goes out to Jayme Moye. I have not failed to appreciate where I have "caught" her in her career. She is already an award-winning journalist and on her way to becoming a world-class author. All enjoyable reading in this book is her doing. Anything awkward, or downright tough to read, I would be to blame. Jayme's ability to interview me for an hour and then put to paper stories from my fragmented memory is astonishing, not to mention the fact that she joined me and Fiona Thornewill on my 100th ascent of the Nose, as the "embedded journalist." Jayme rocks (and yes, that may only be two words, but it is a complete sentence).

Steve Edwards, you are gone but not forgotten. Thanks for teaching me that a person can do something mediocre, something hard, or something great, but when you attempt something that's so challenging that you yourself have doubts about completing it, then that's rad. I'm going for 200.

ABOUT THE AUTHORS

In addition to his climbing accolades, **Hans Florine** is the coauthor of *Speed Climbing* and has contributed to three other books, as well as written articles for *Rock & Ice* and *Climbing* magazines. Hans served as executive director of the American Sport Climbers Federation from 1992 to 1996 and is currently an Ambassador for the Access Fund, as well as manager and shareholder at Touchstone Climbing & Fitness, the largest climbing-gym chain in the country. He lives in the San Francisco Bay Area and maintains strong relationships, fund-raising and otherwise, with Yosemite Conservancy, Outward Bound, the Access Fund, the American Safe Climbing Association, American Alpine Club, Sierra Club, and NatureBridge. He is also a professional motivational speaker, delivering keynotes at trade shows, conferences, and college auditoriums worldwide, from local Rotary club meetings to Fortune 500 events.

Jayme Moye is an award-winning freelance journalist based in Boulder, Colorado, and the former managing editor of *Elevation Outdoors*. She is a regular contributor at *National Geographic Adventure*, *Men's Journal*, and *5280*. Her stories have been anthologized in *The Best Women's Travel Writing*, Volume 10, and *Vignettes and Postcards from Paris*. This is her first book.